Retro Flower

Power Adult Coloring Book

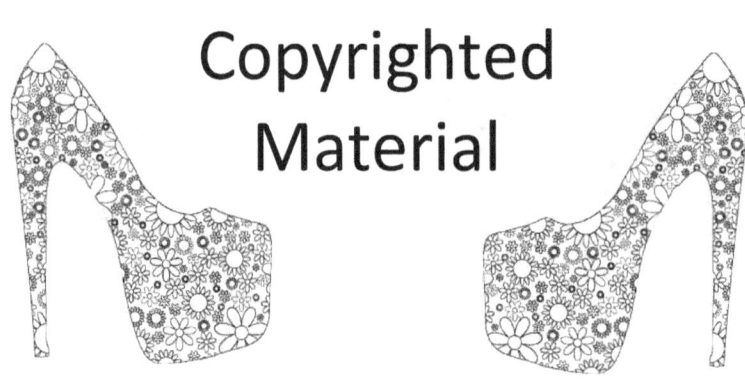

This book belongs to:

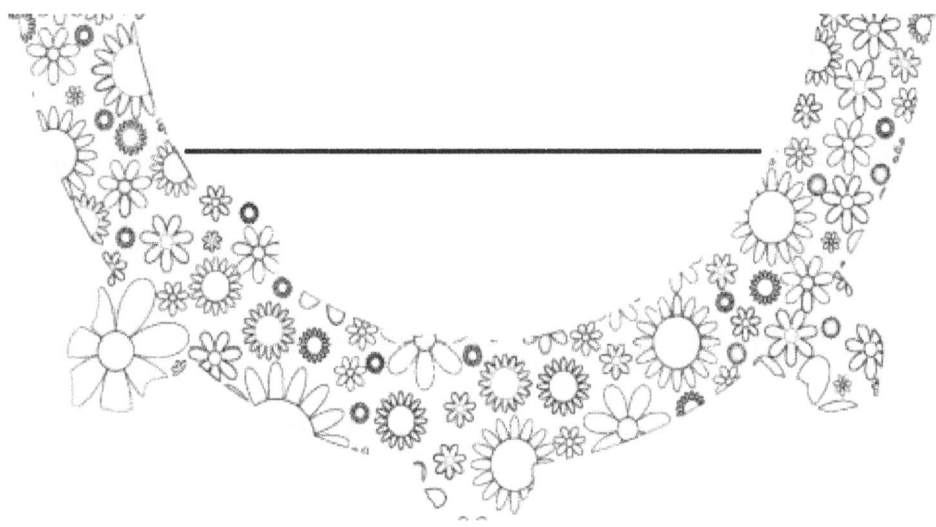

_____

Relax and color the stress away.

Color Test Page

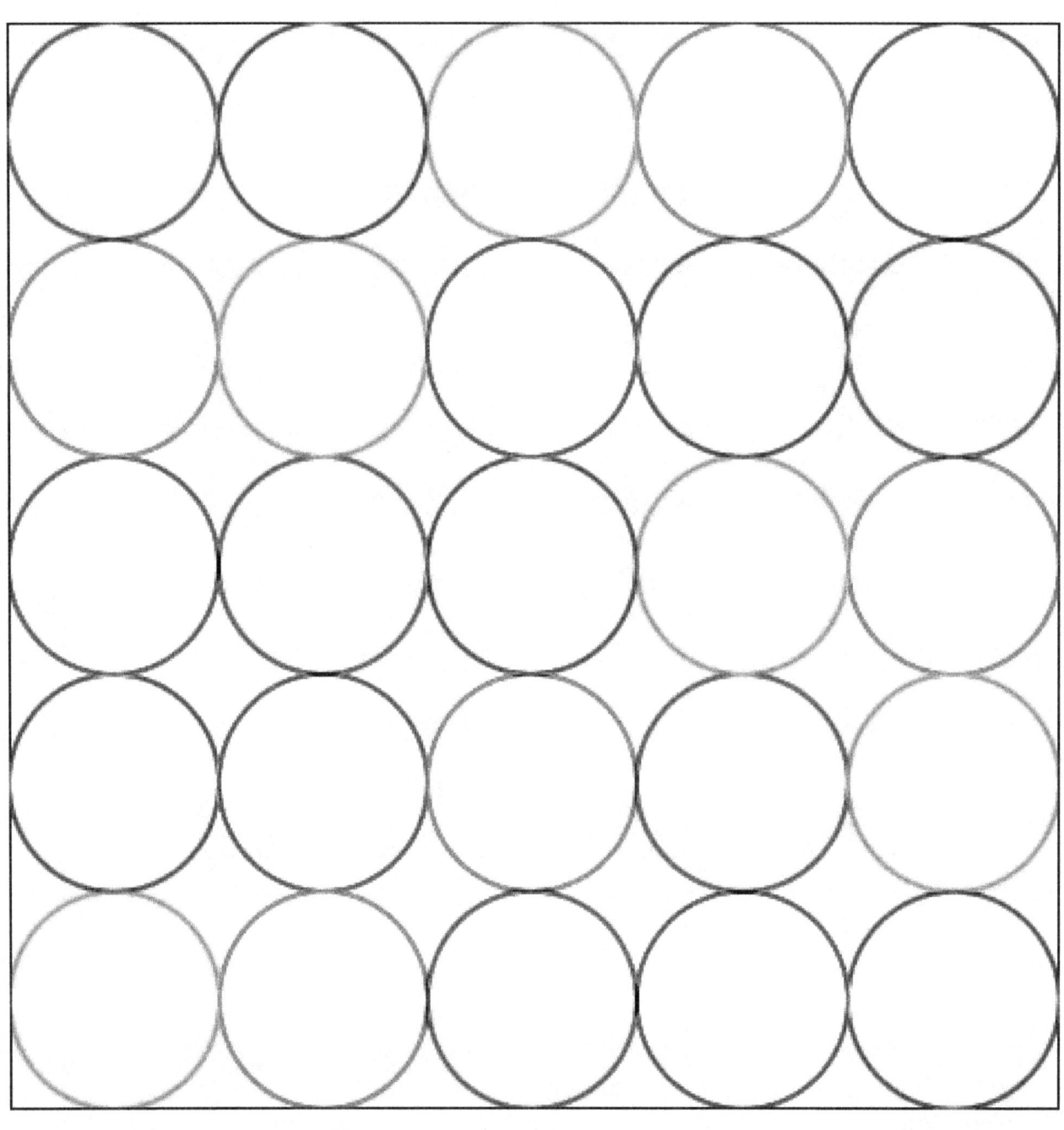

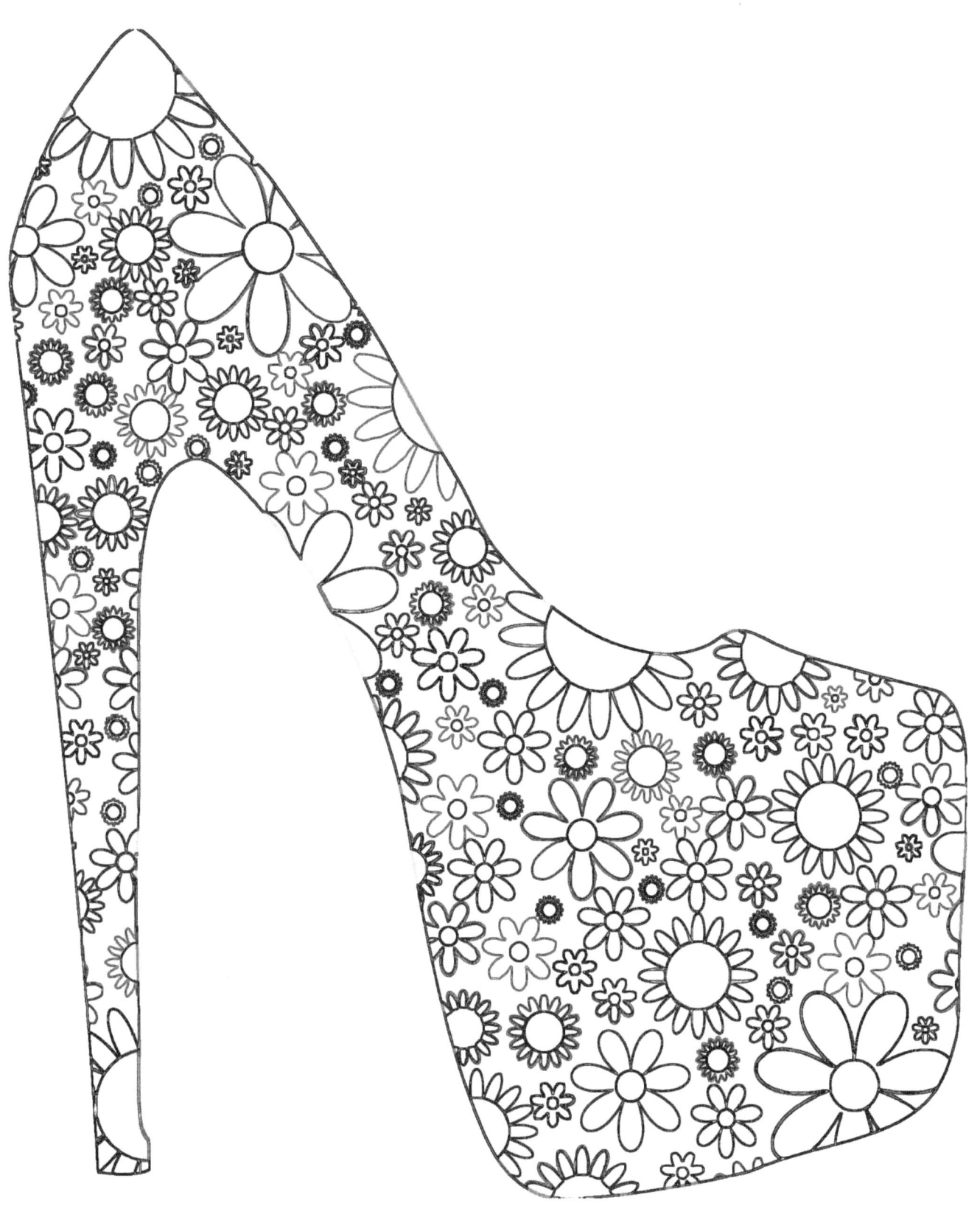

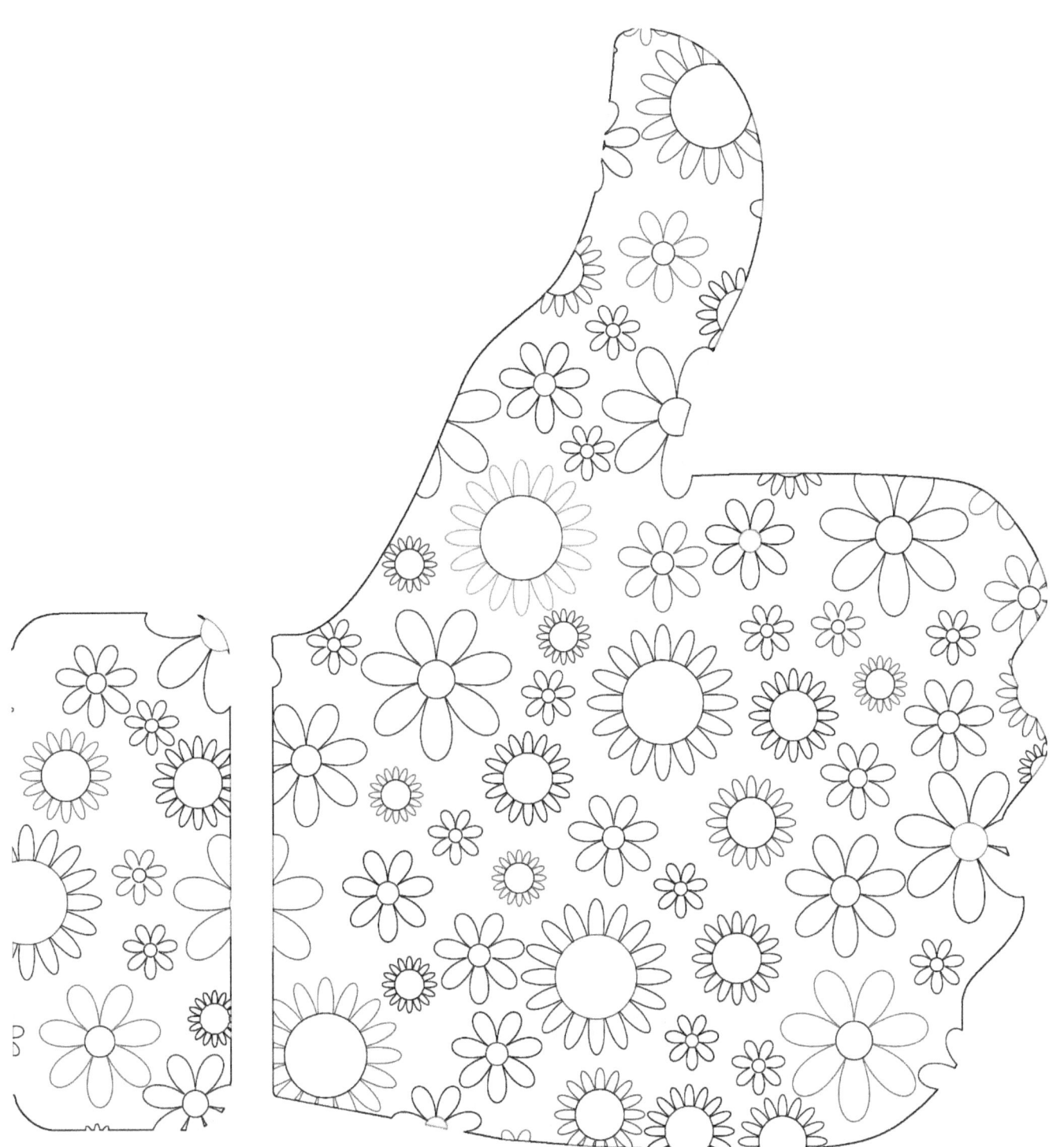

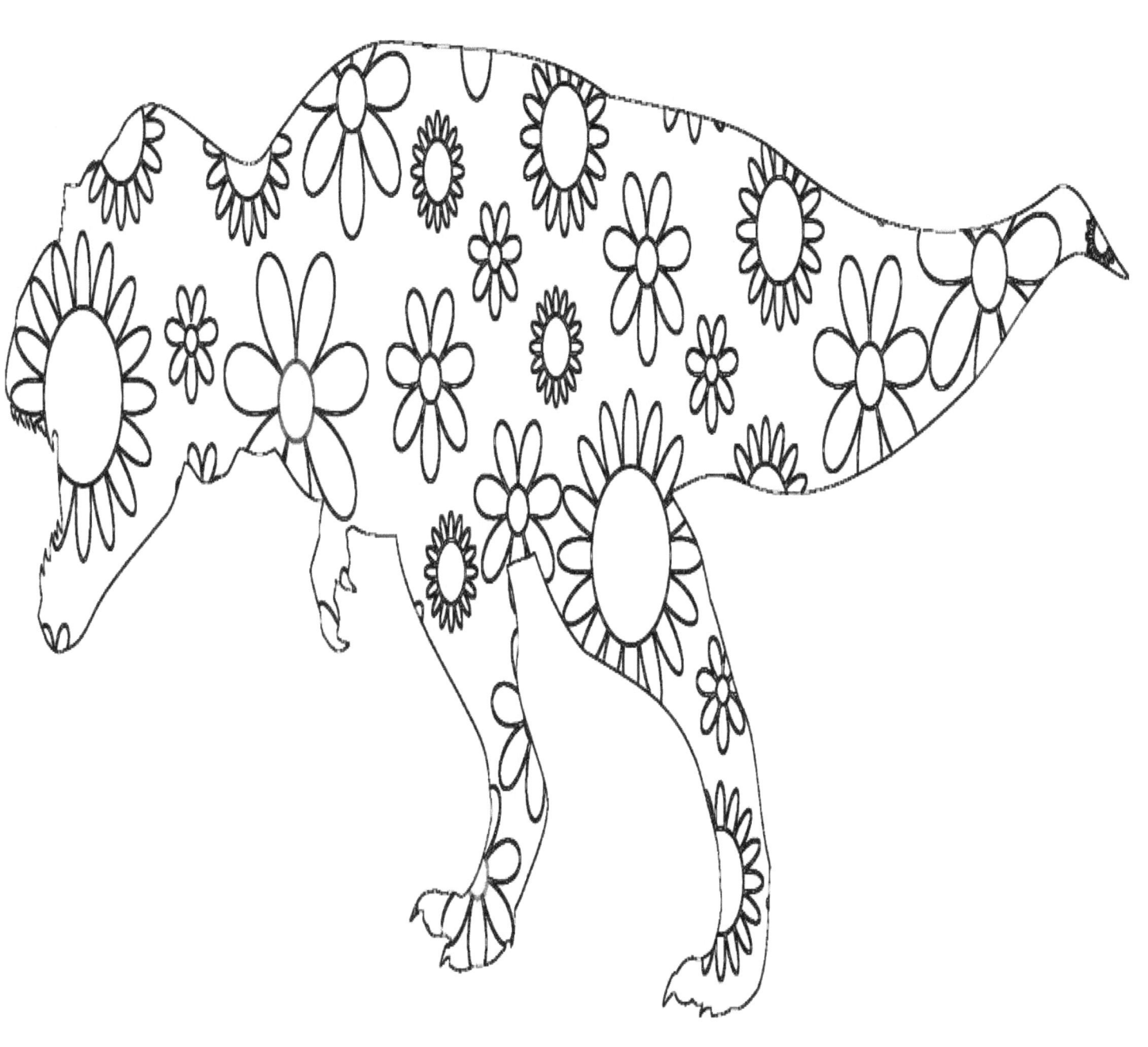

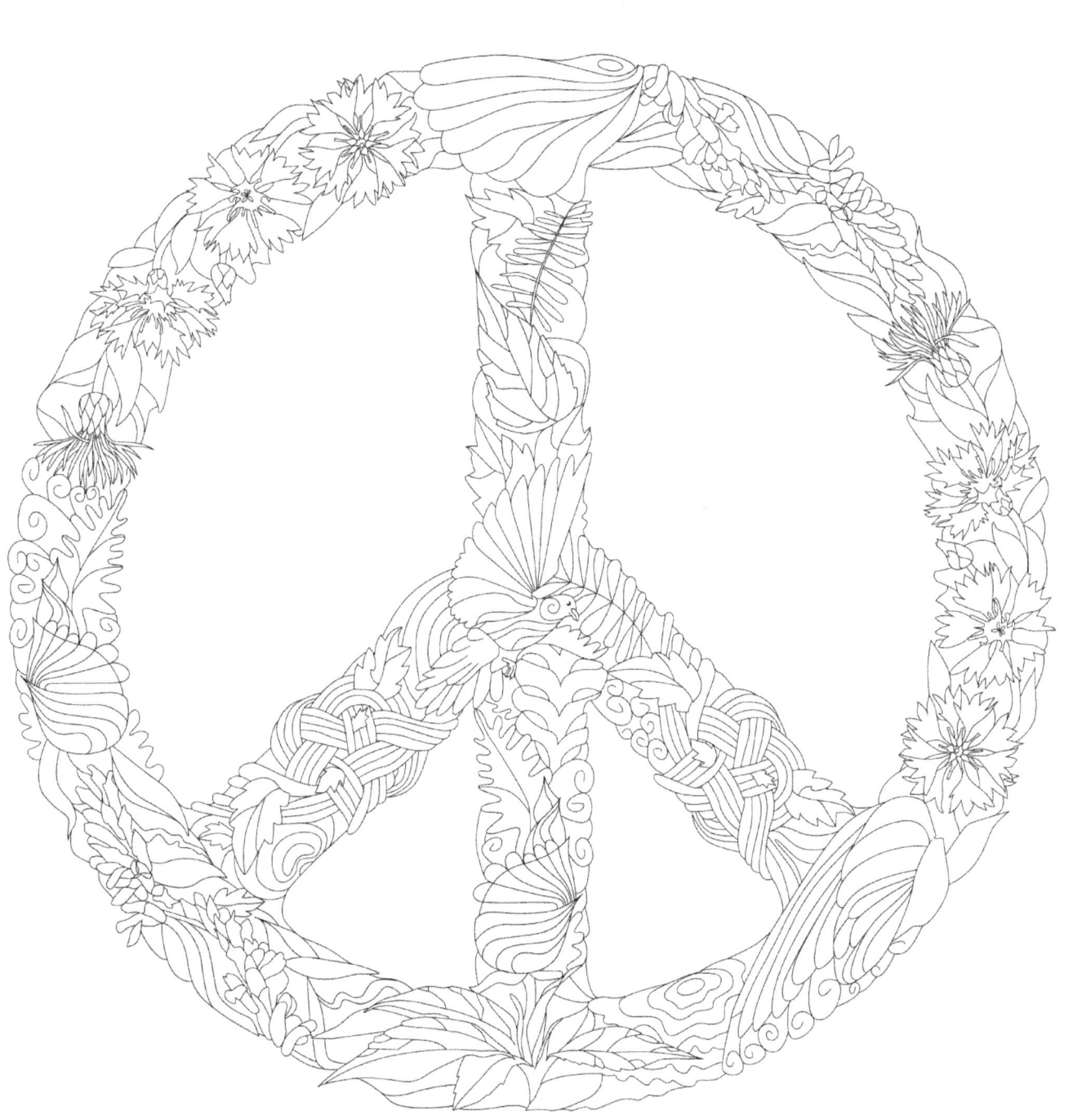

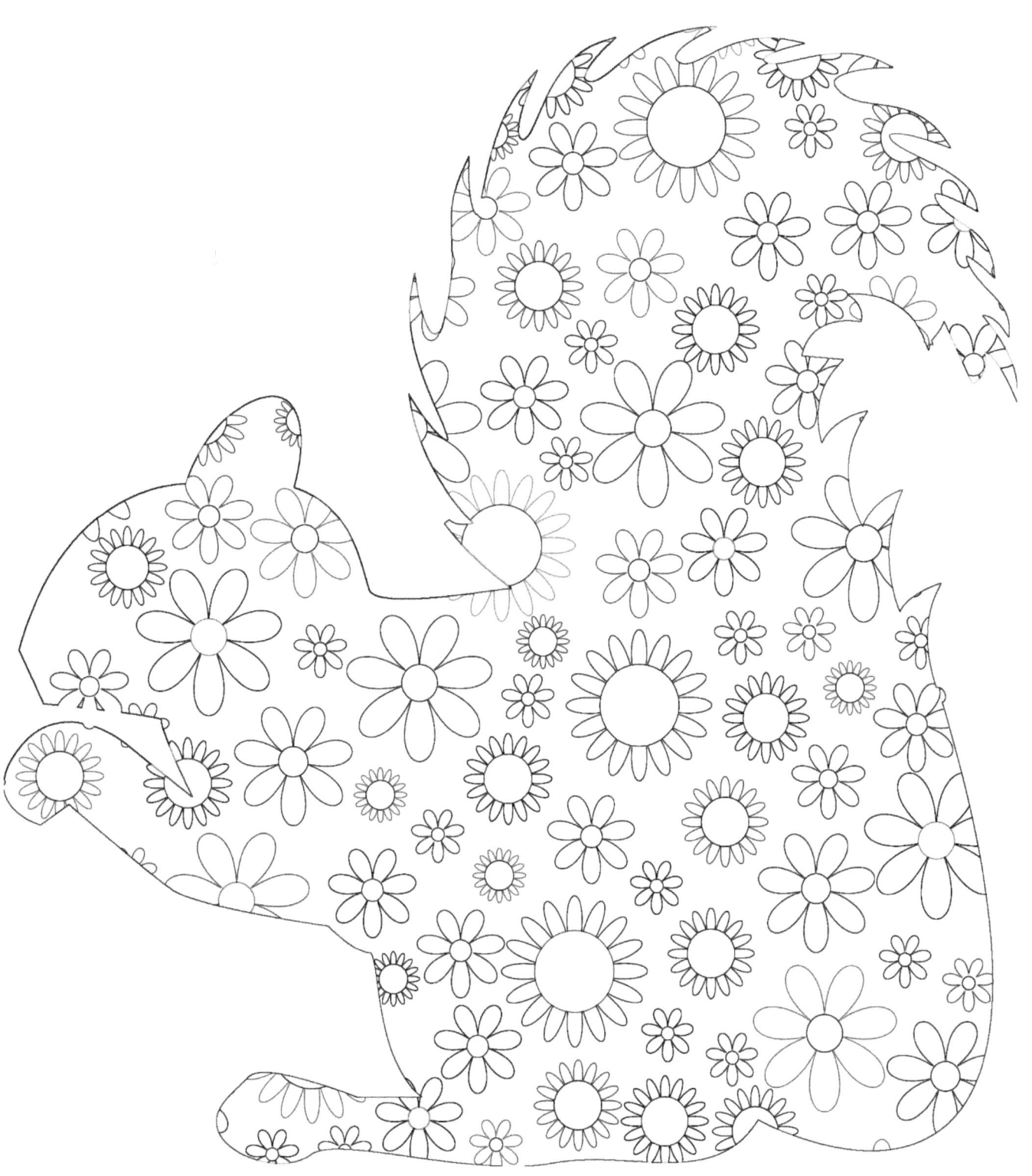

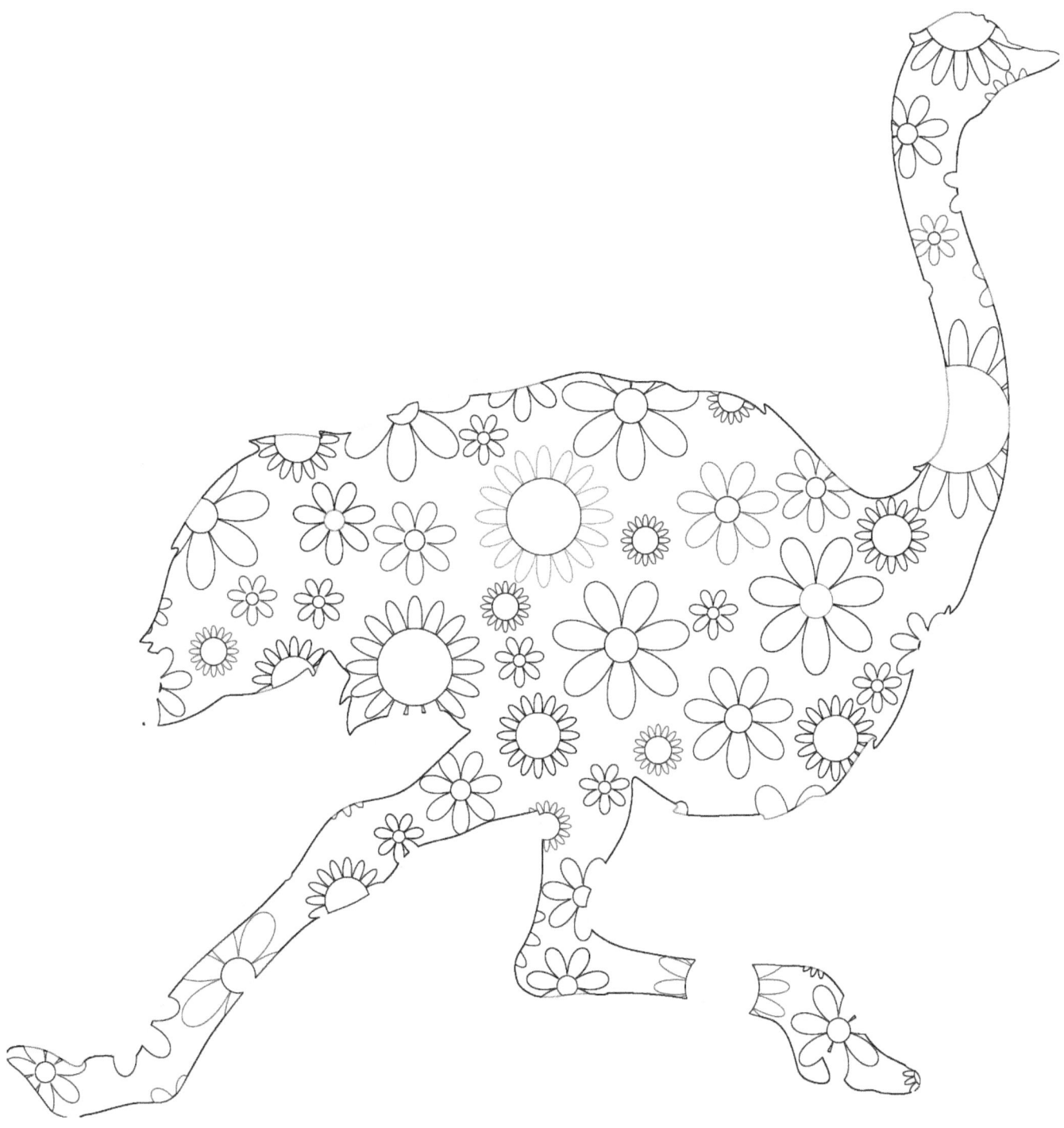

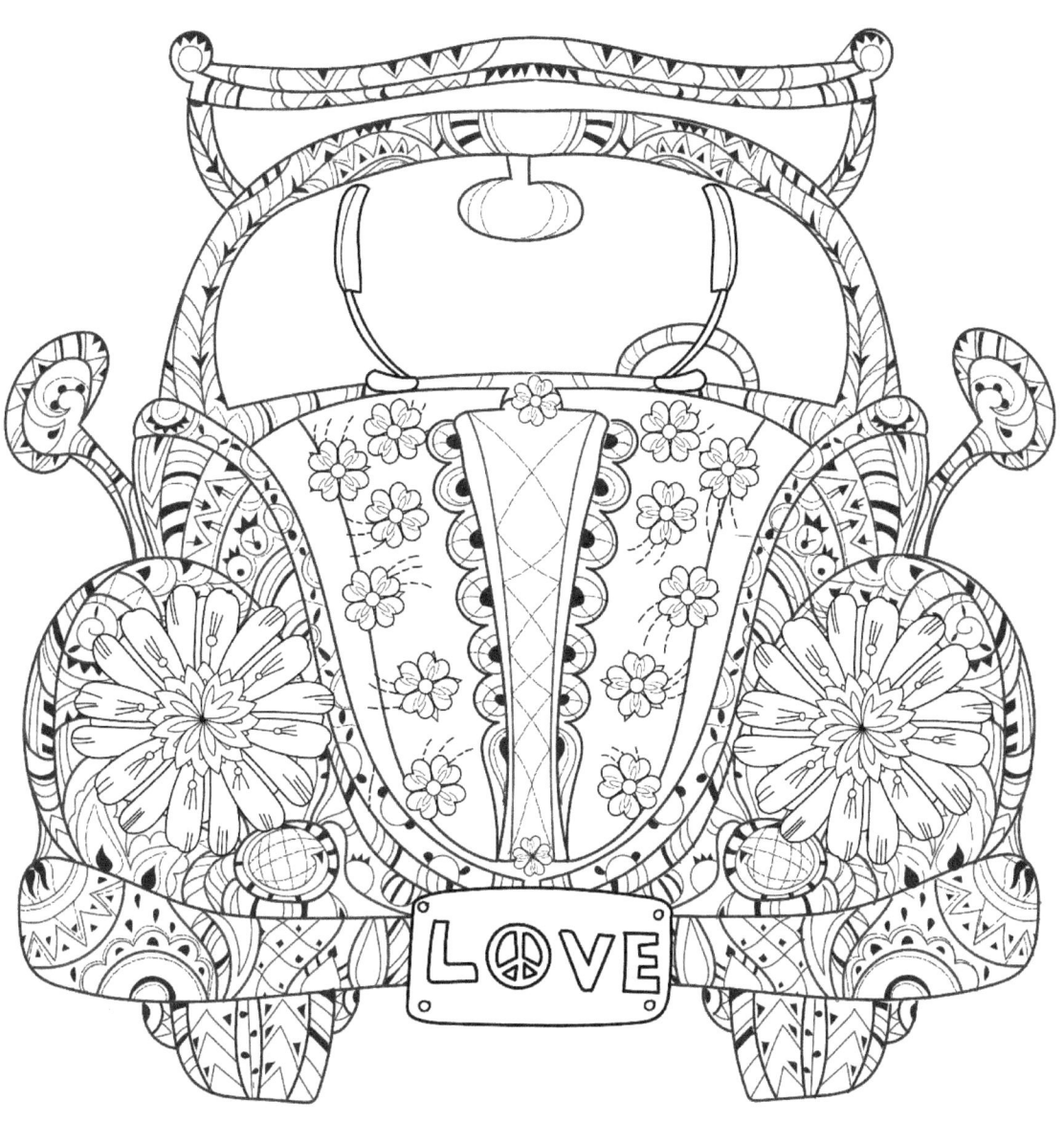

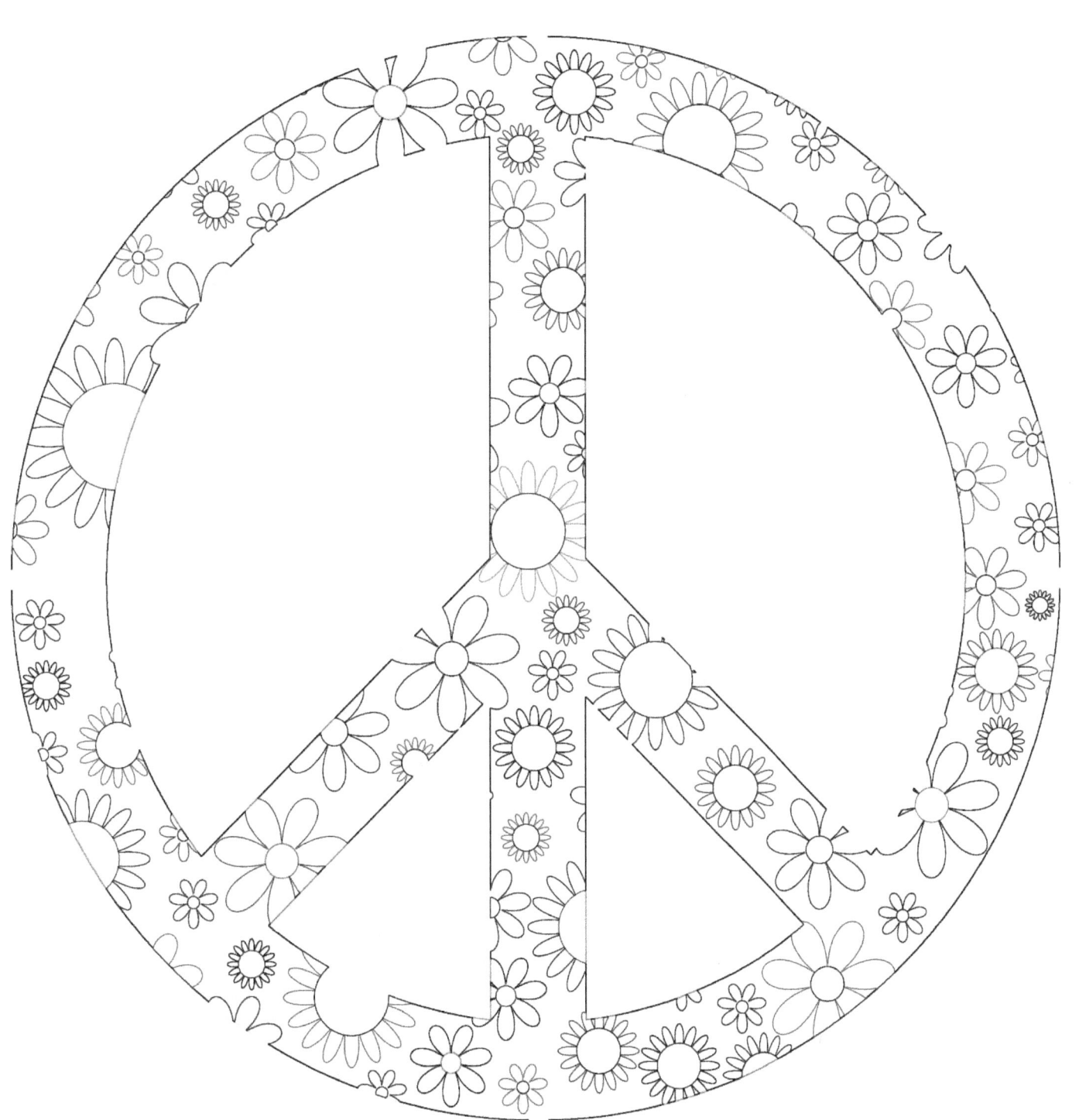

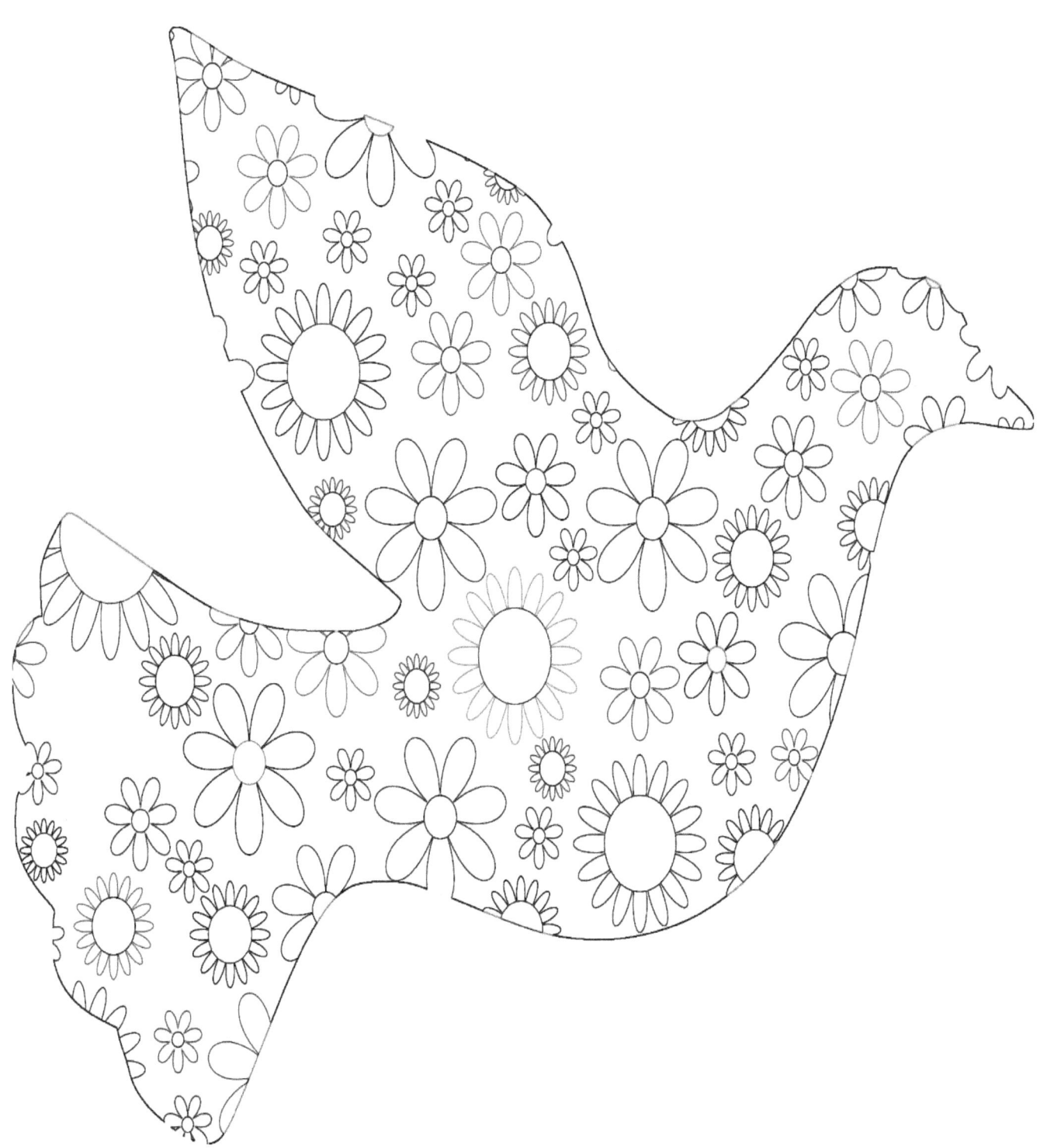

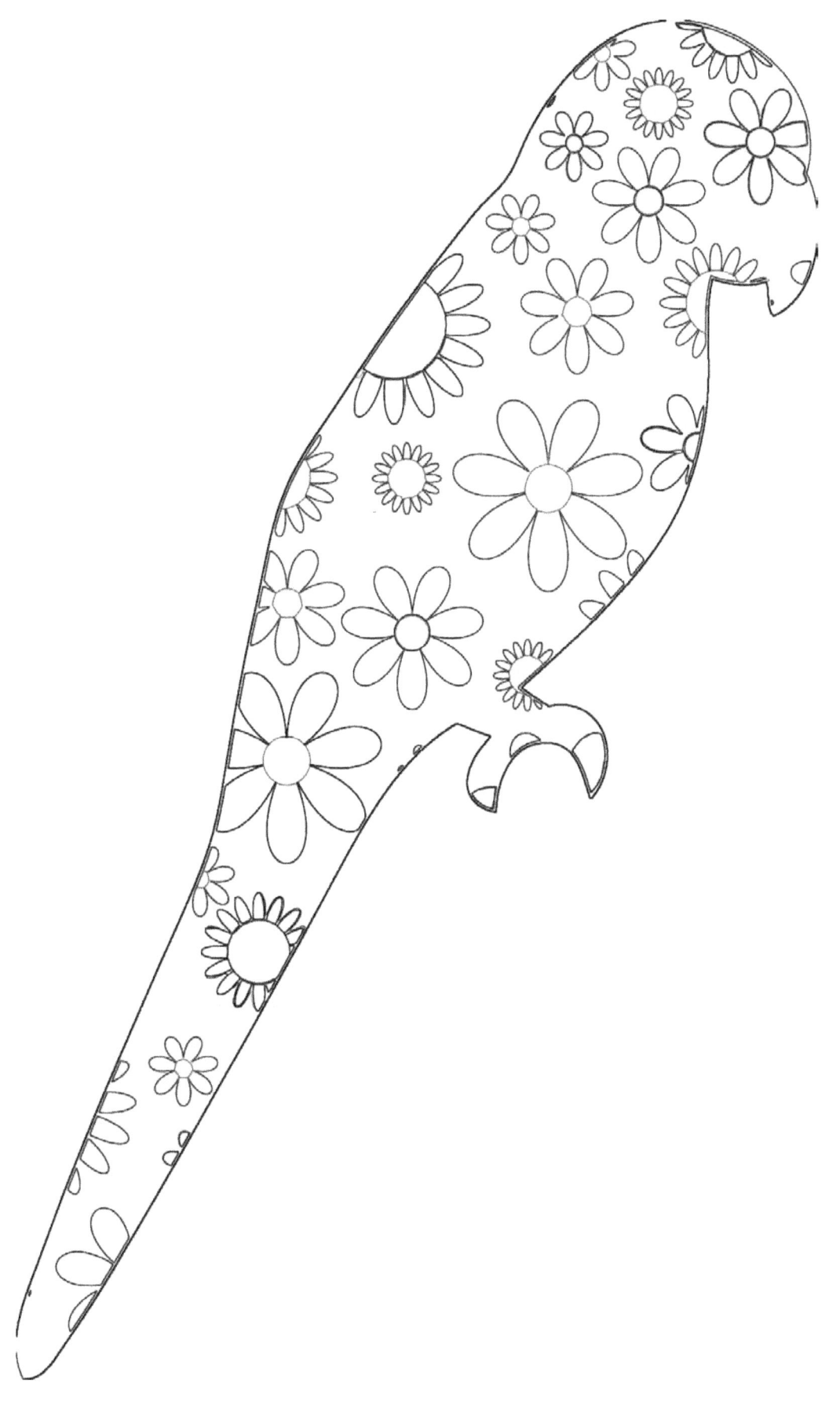

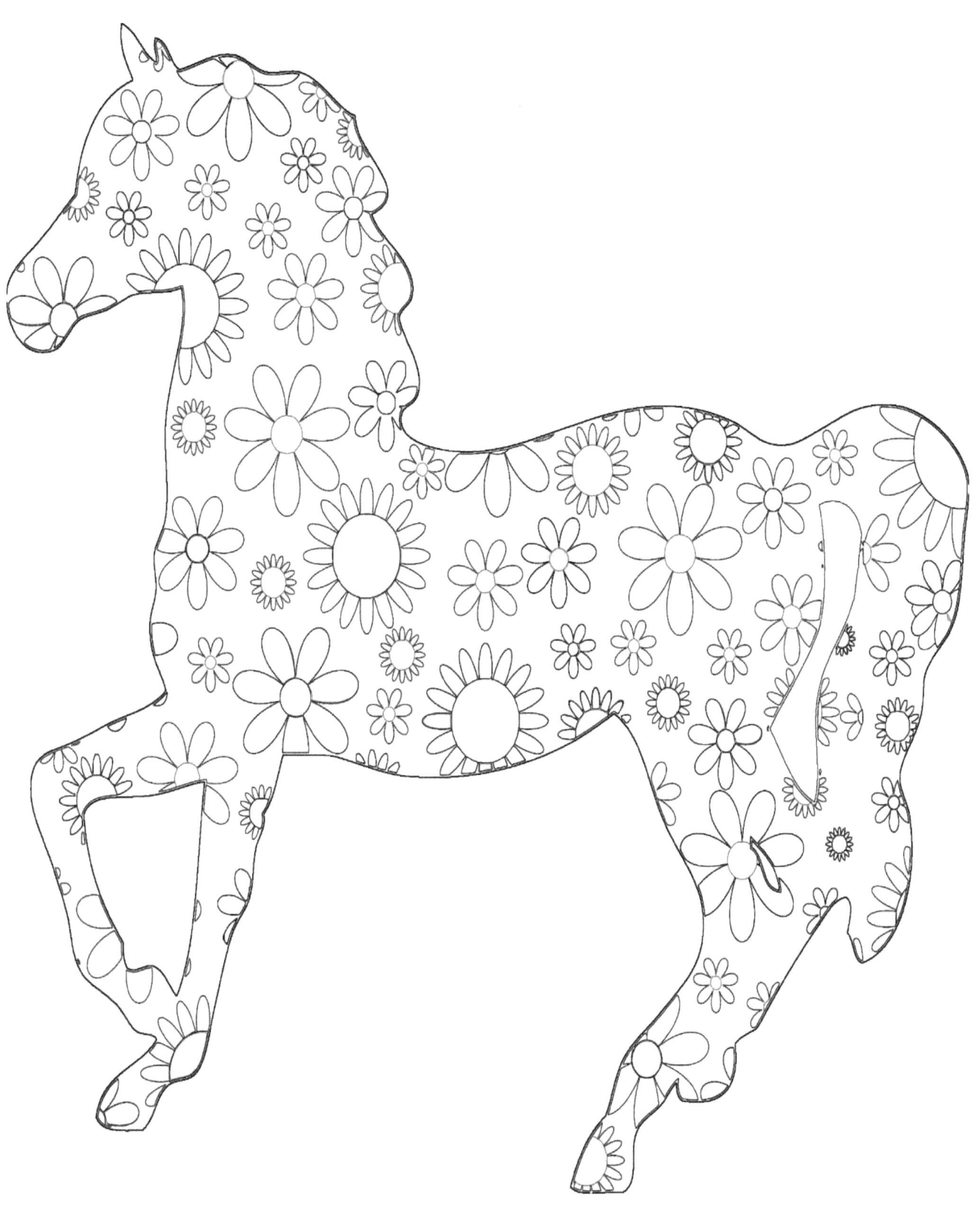

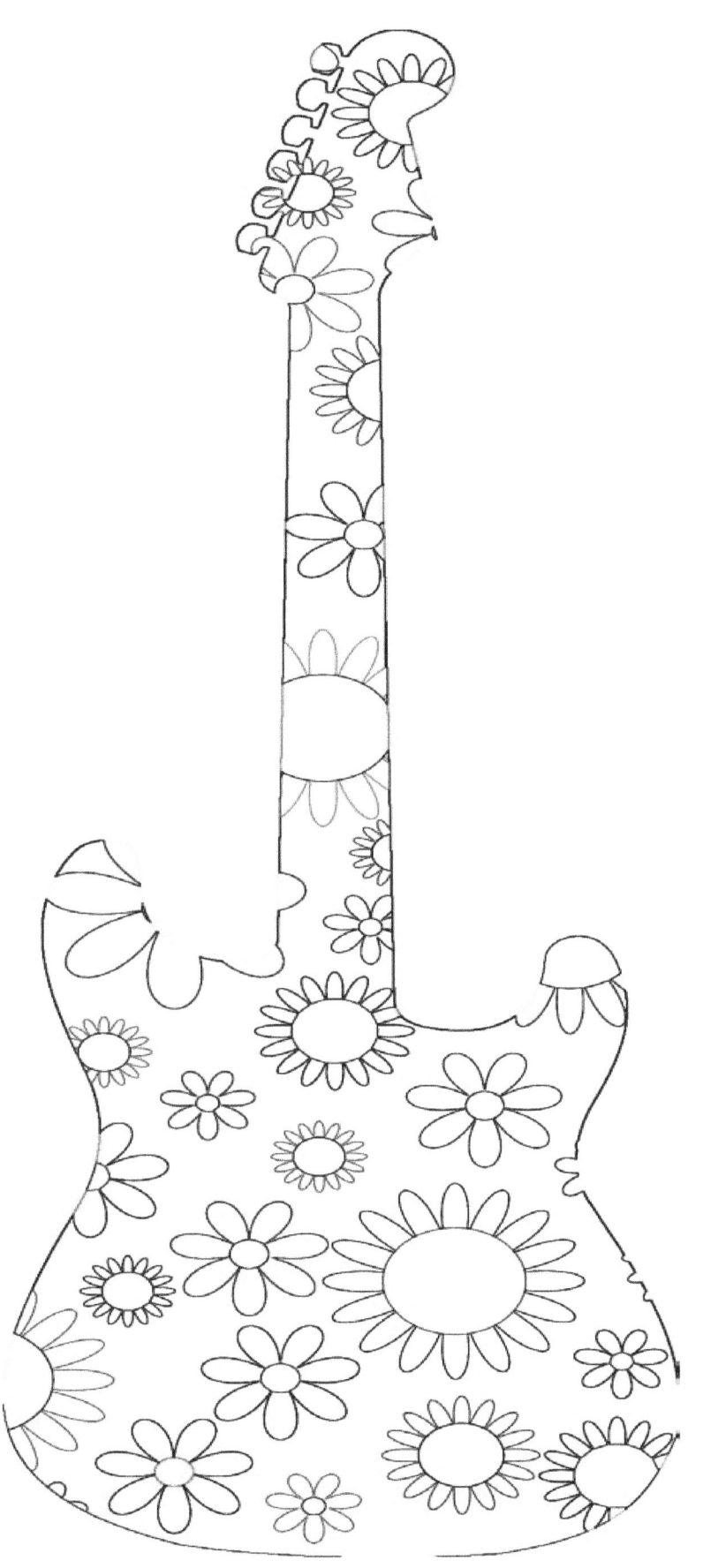

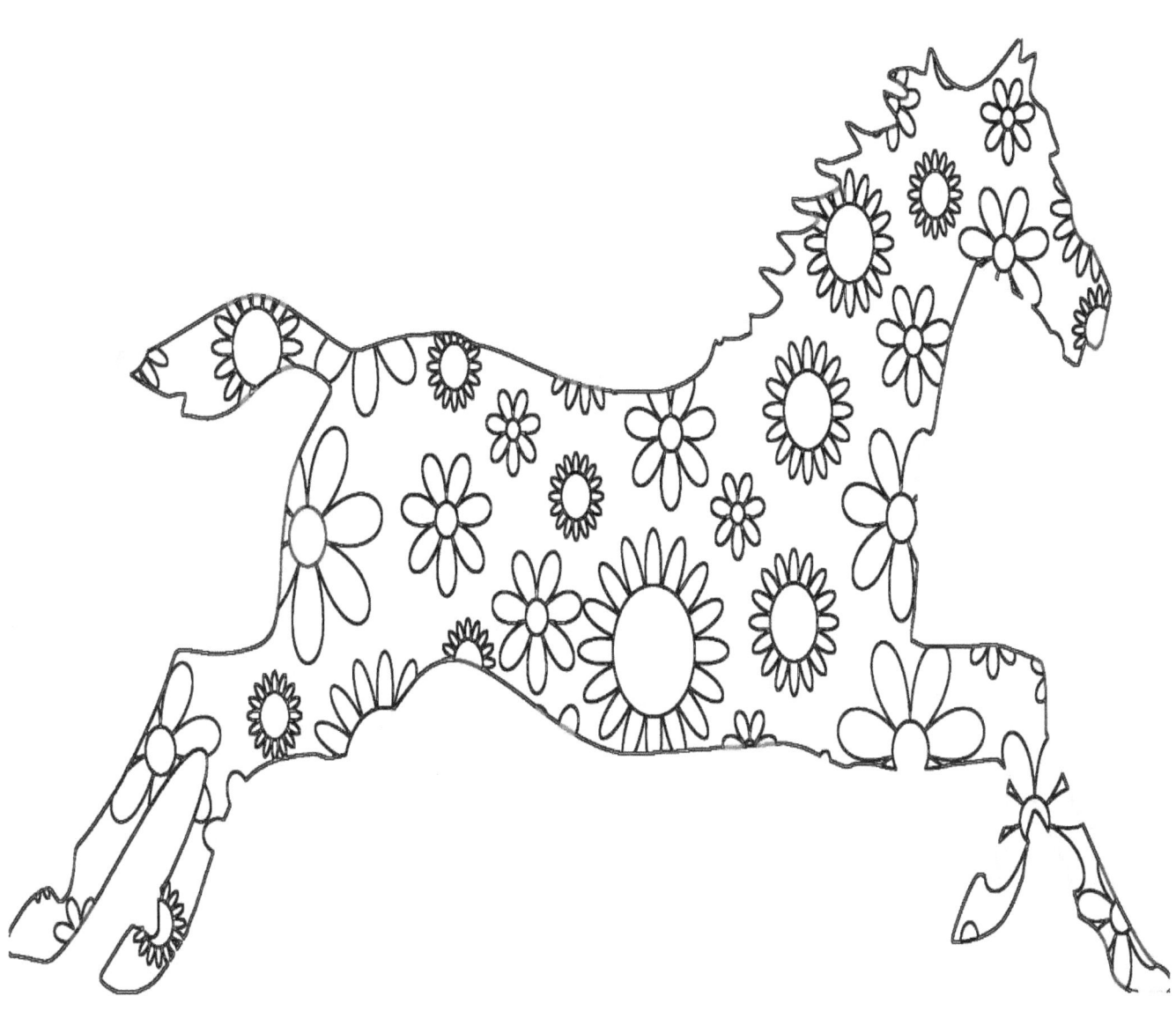

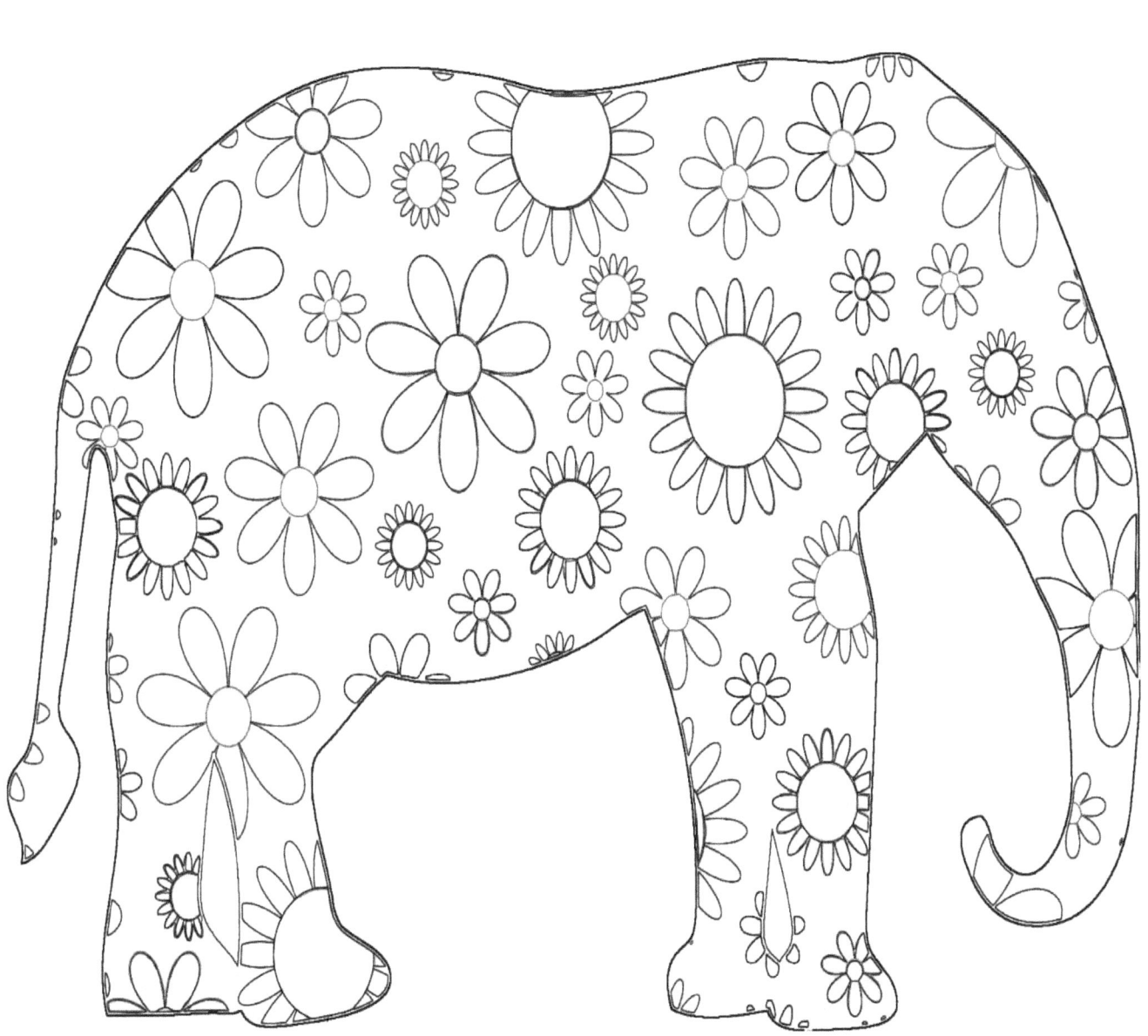

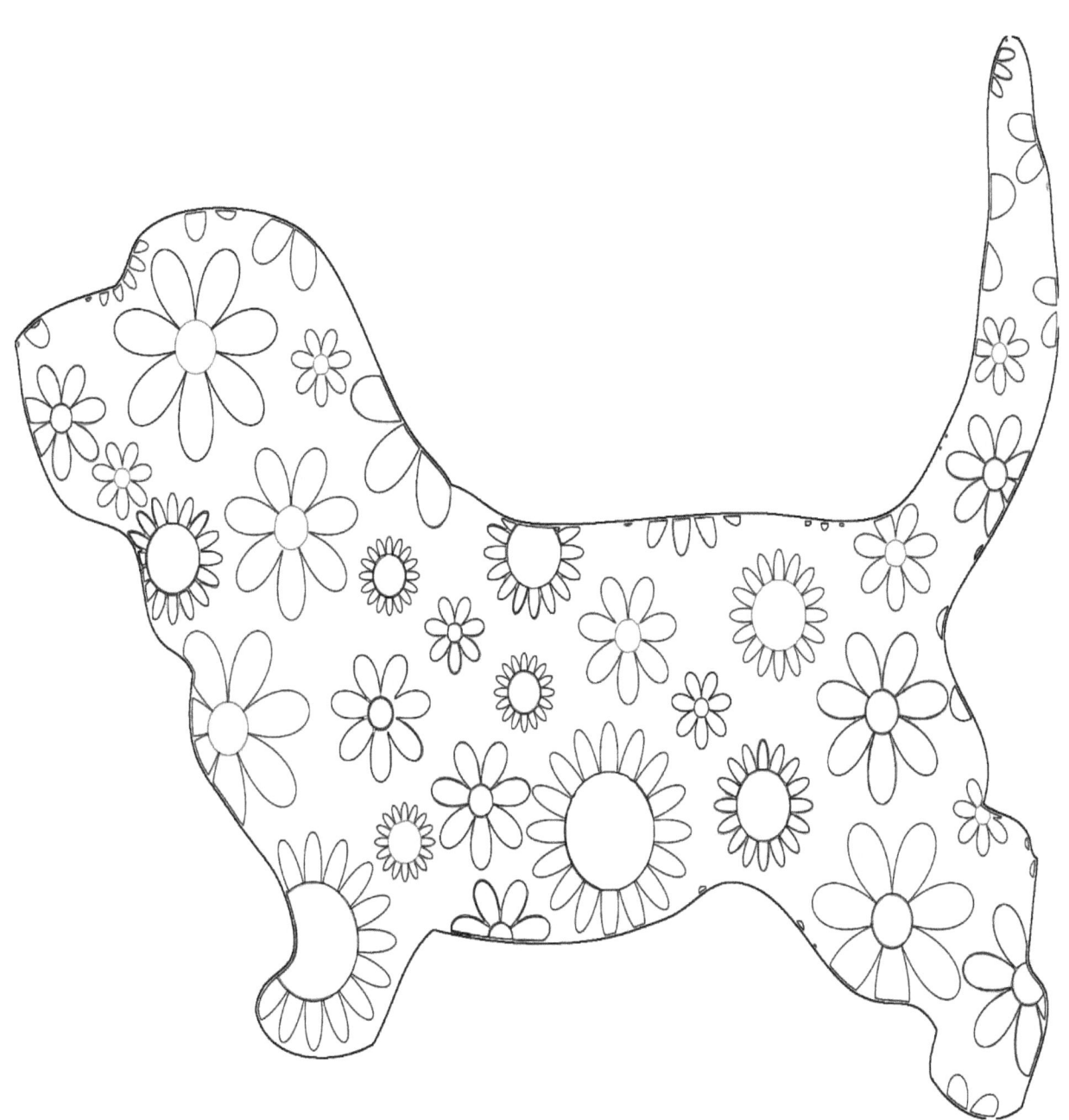

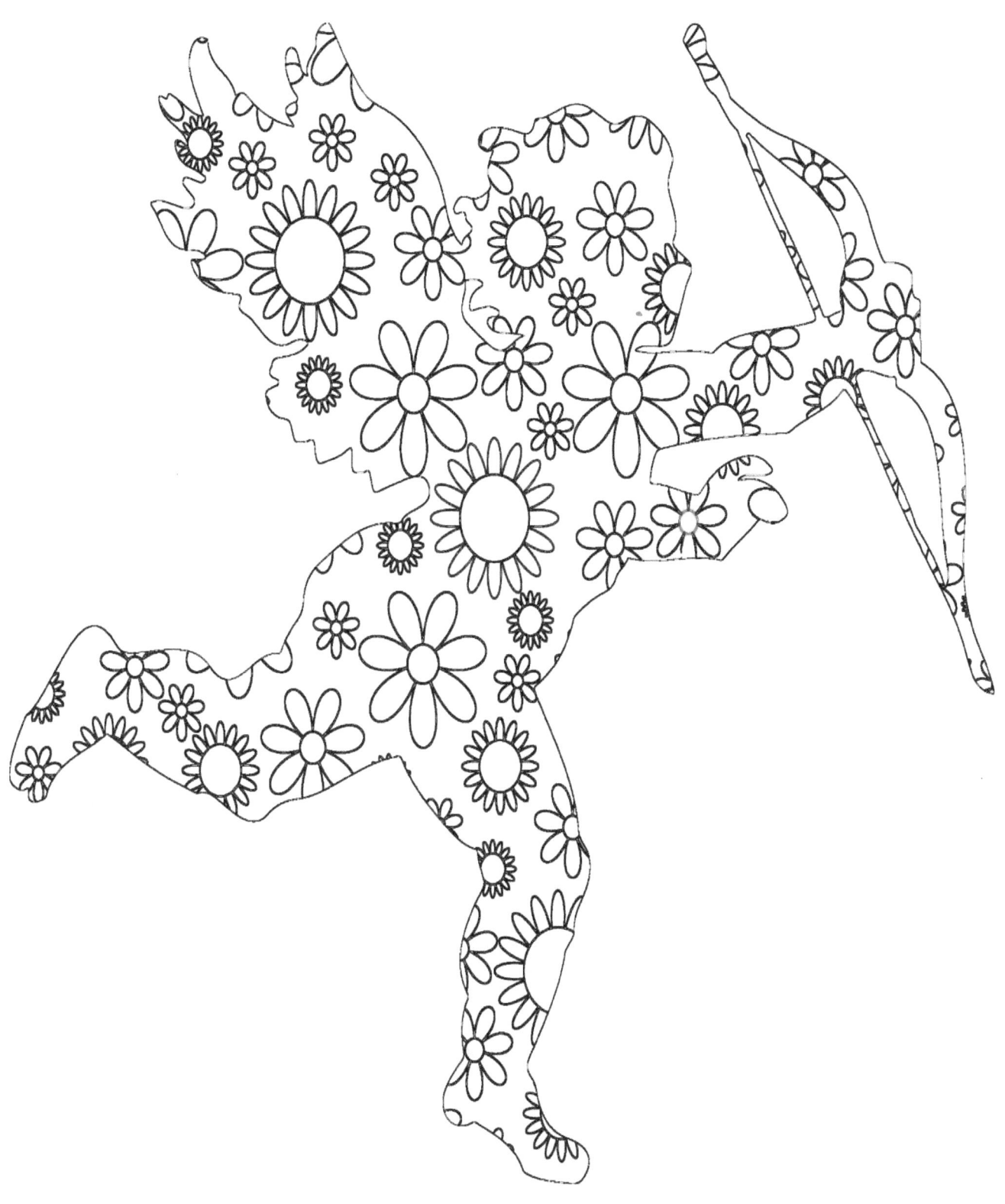

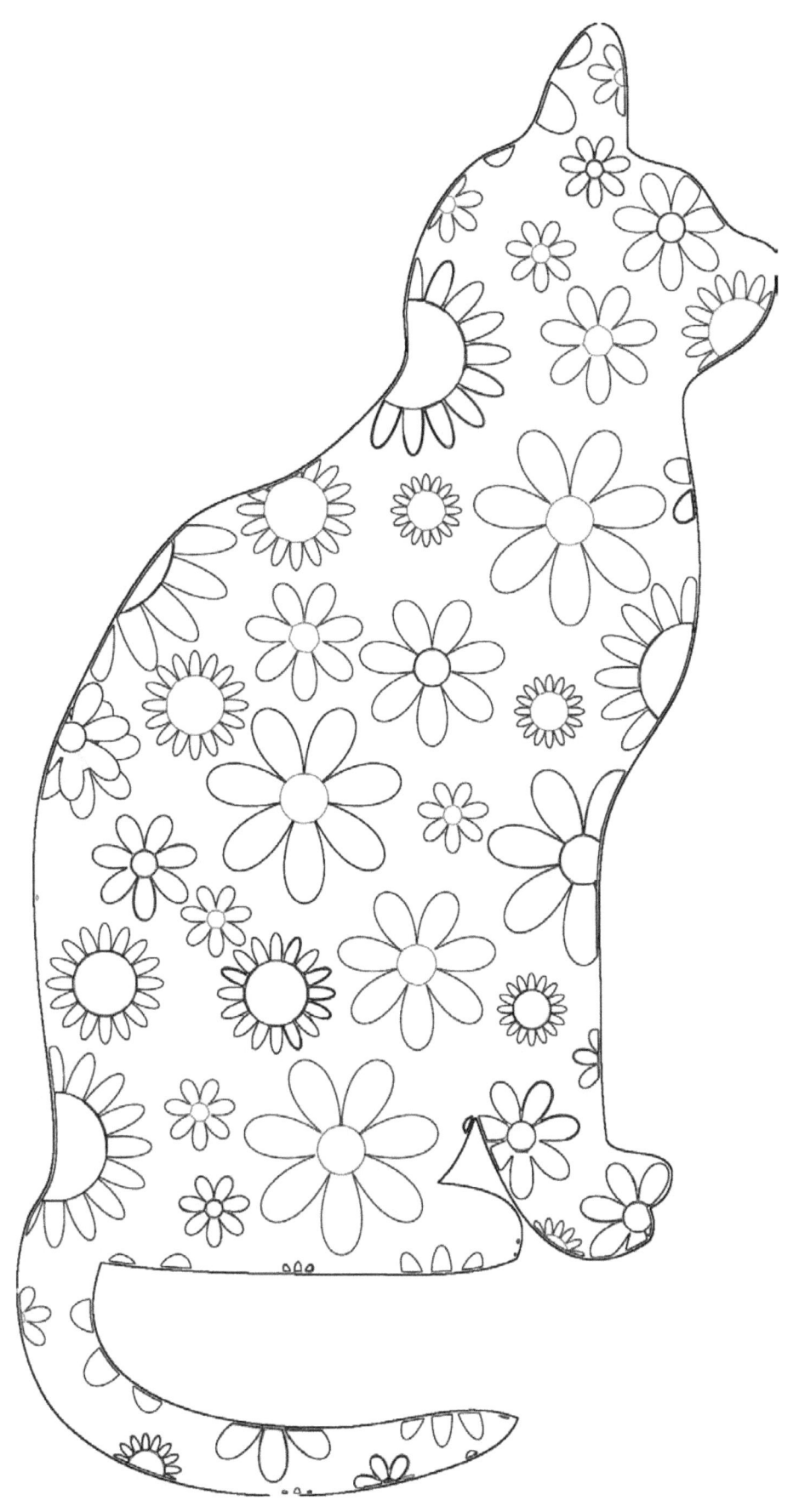

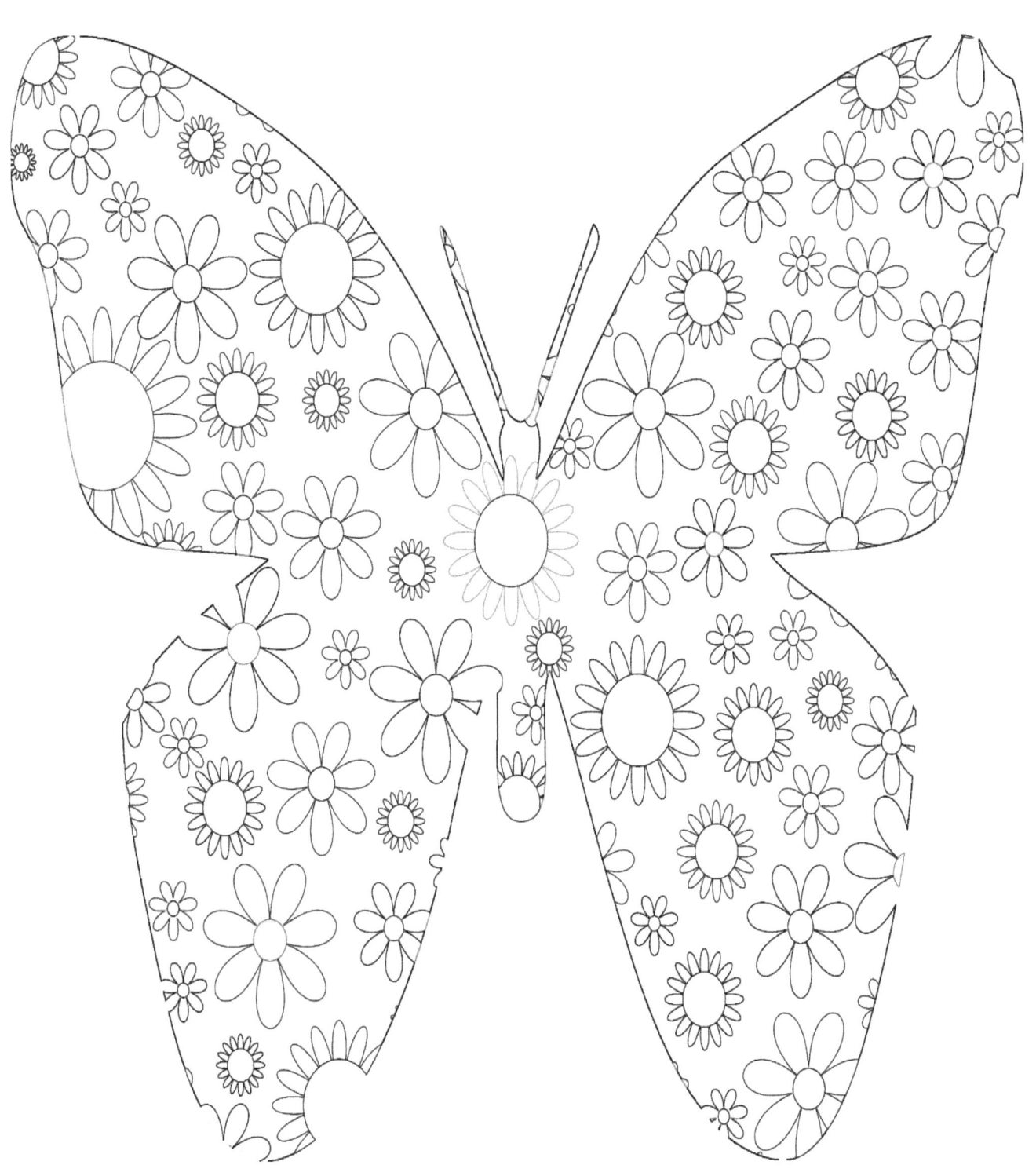

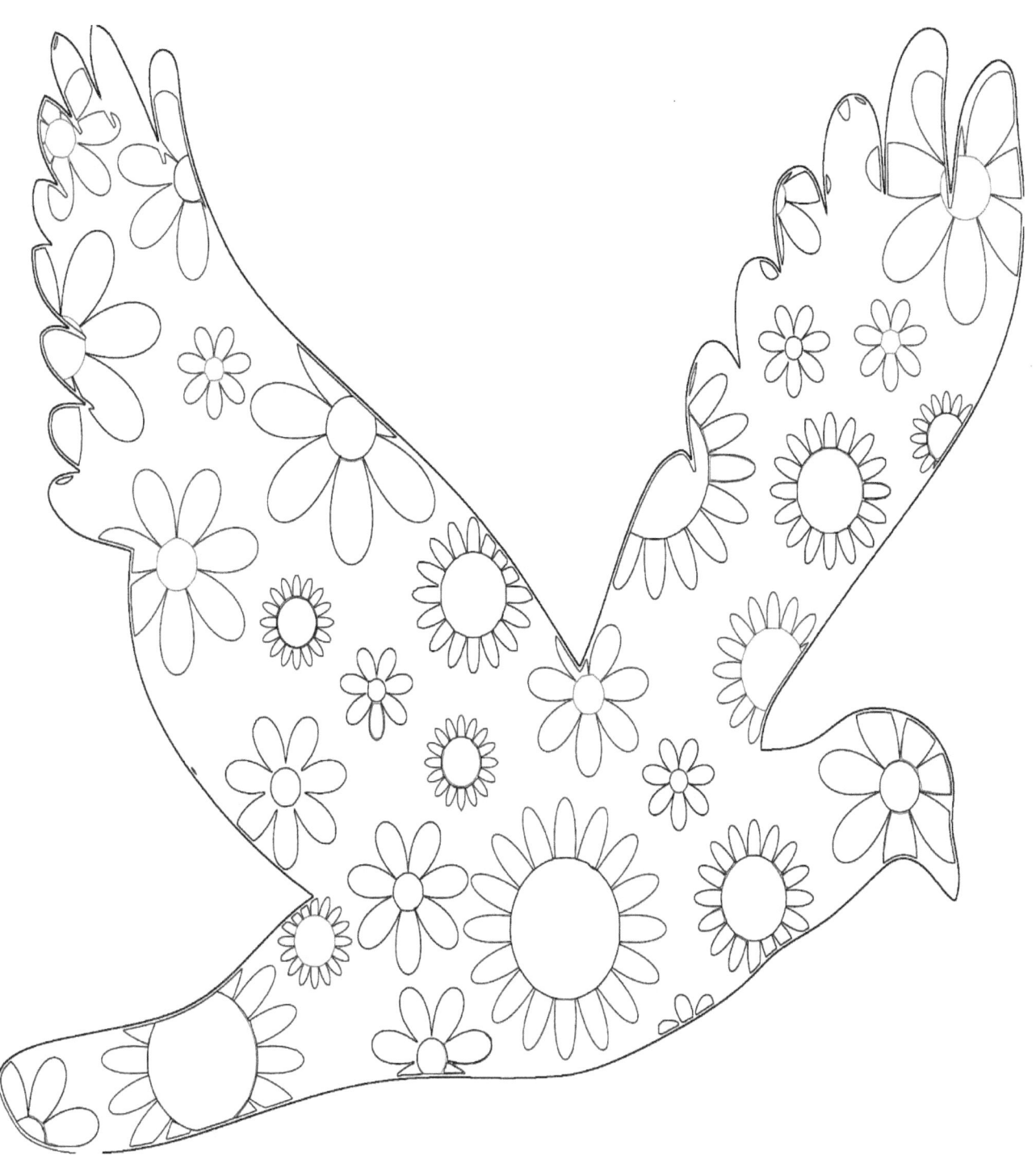

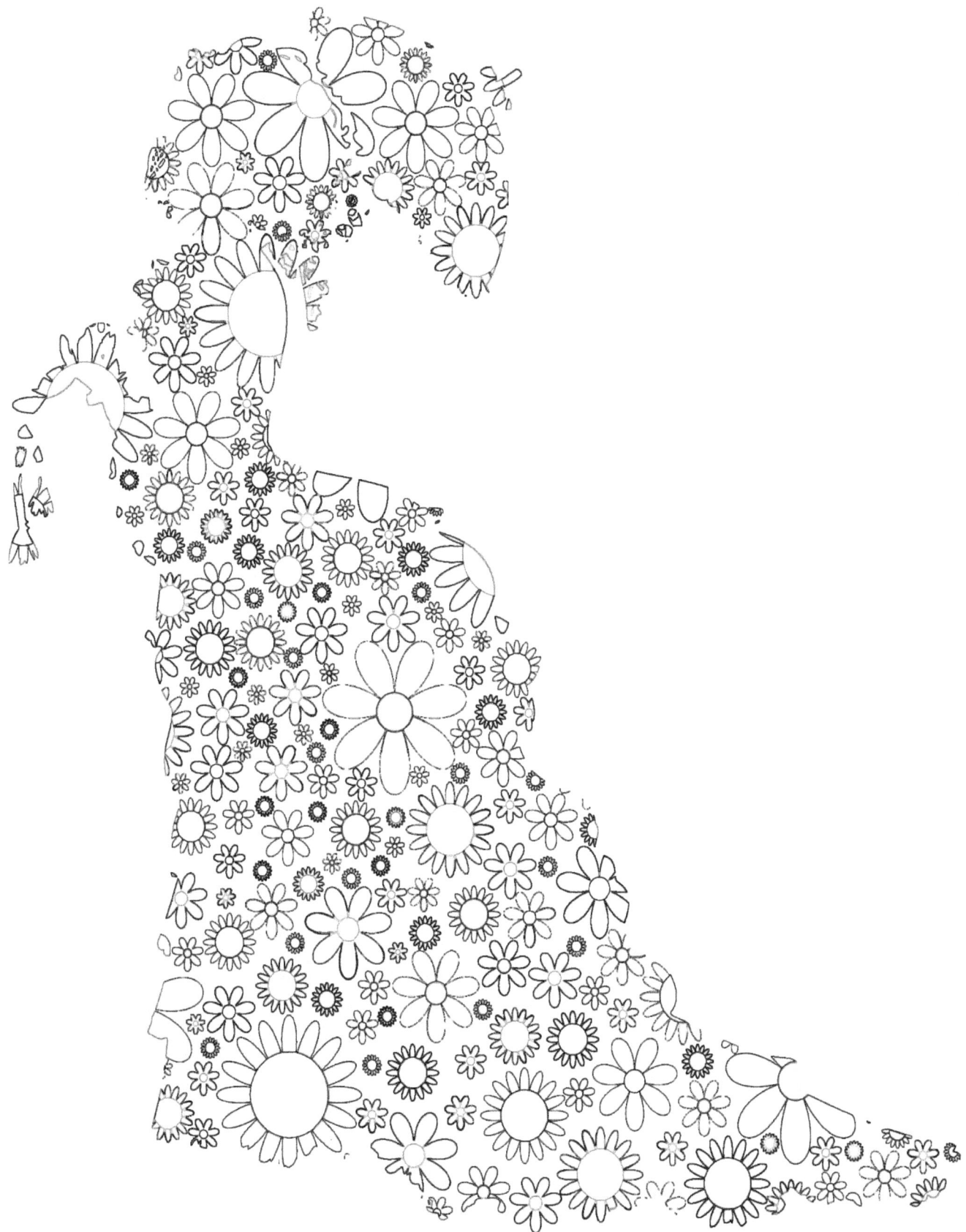

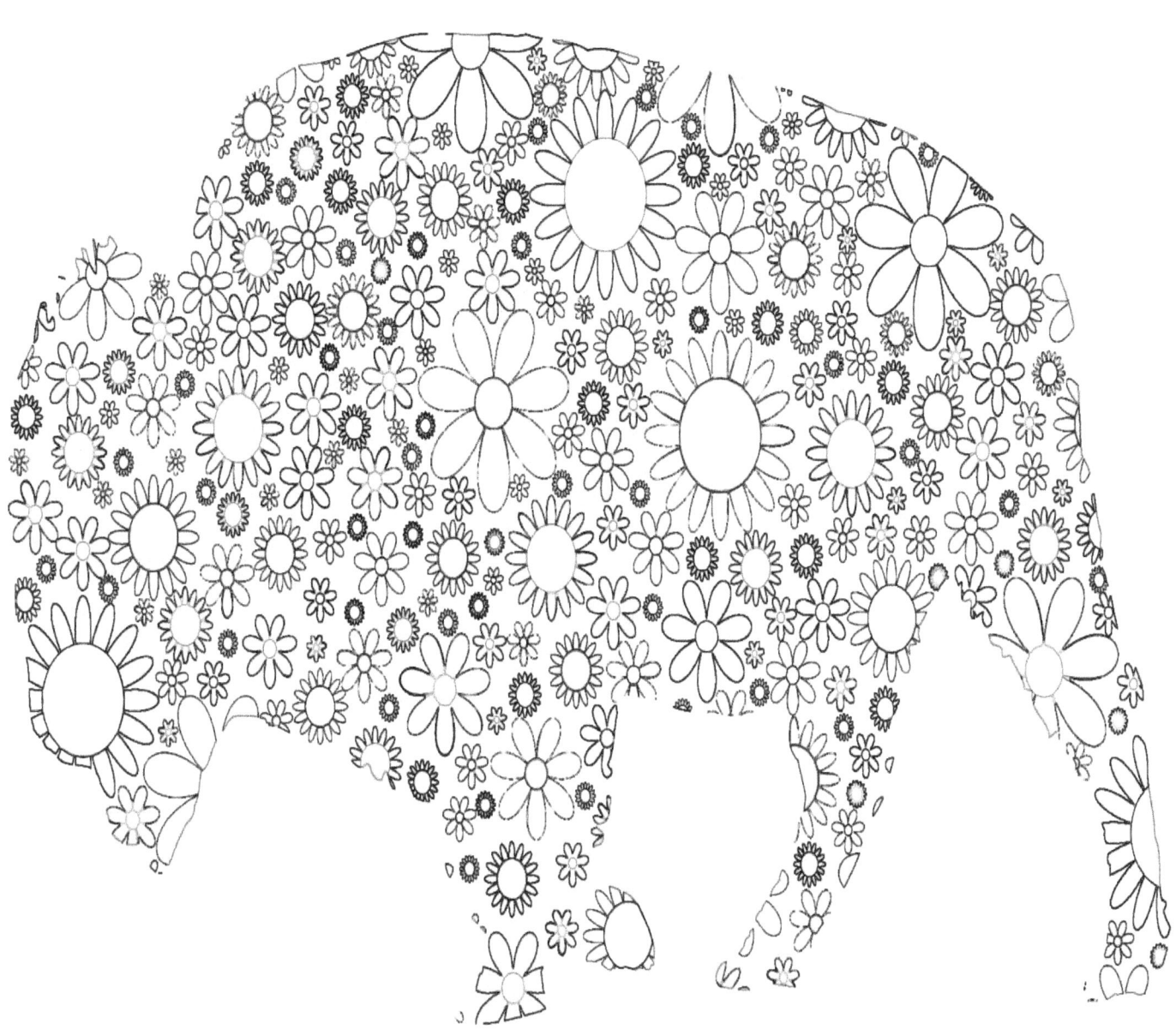

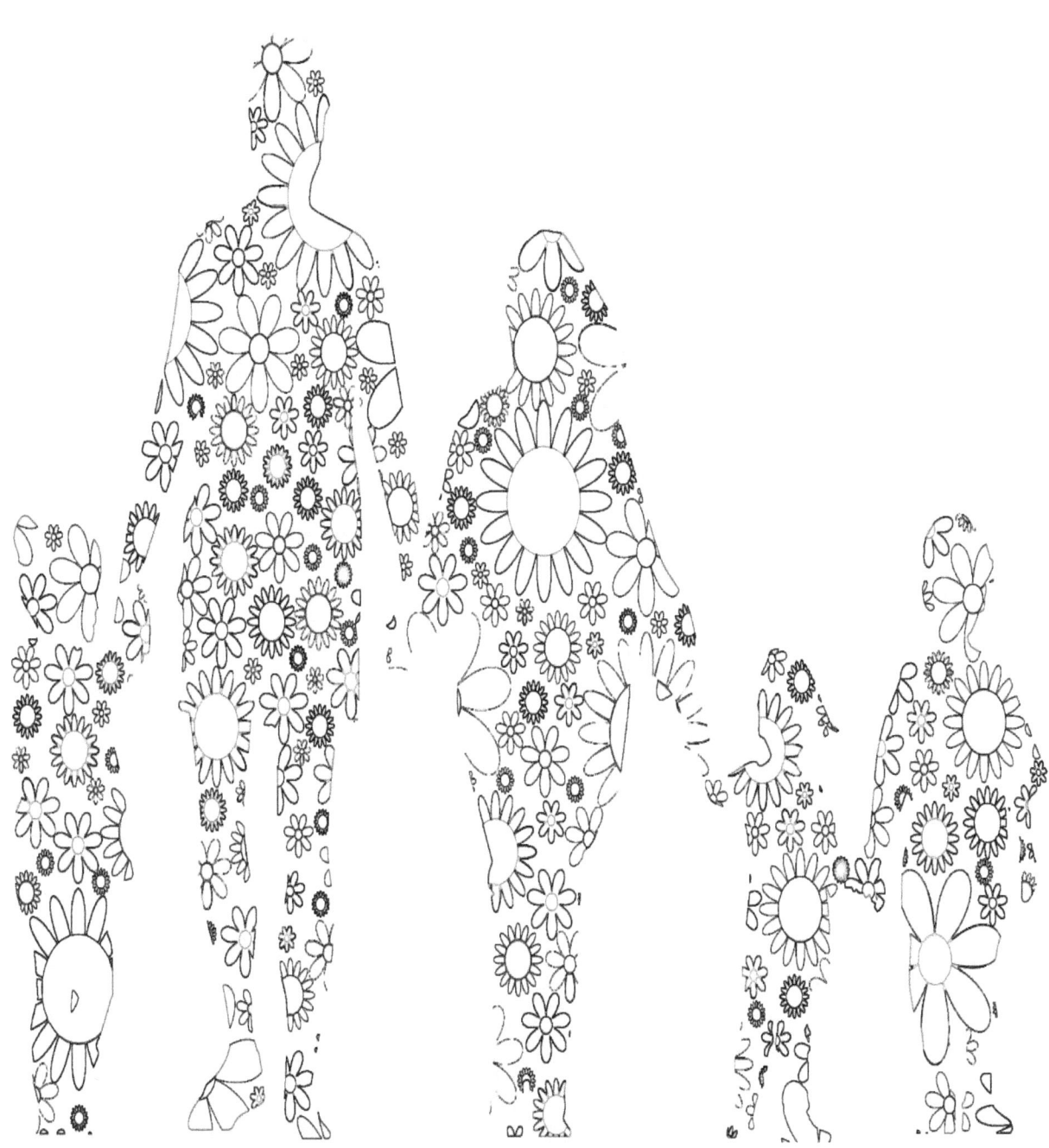

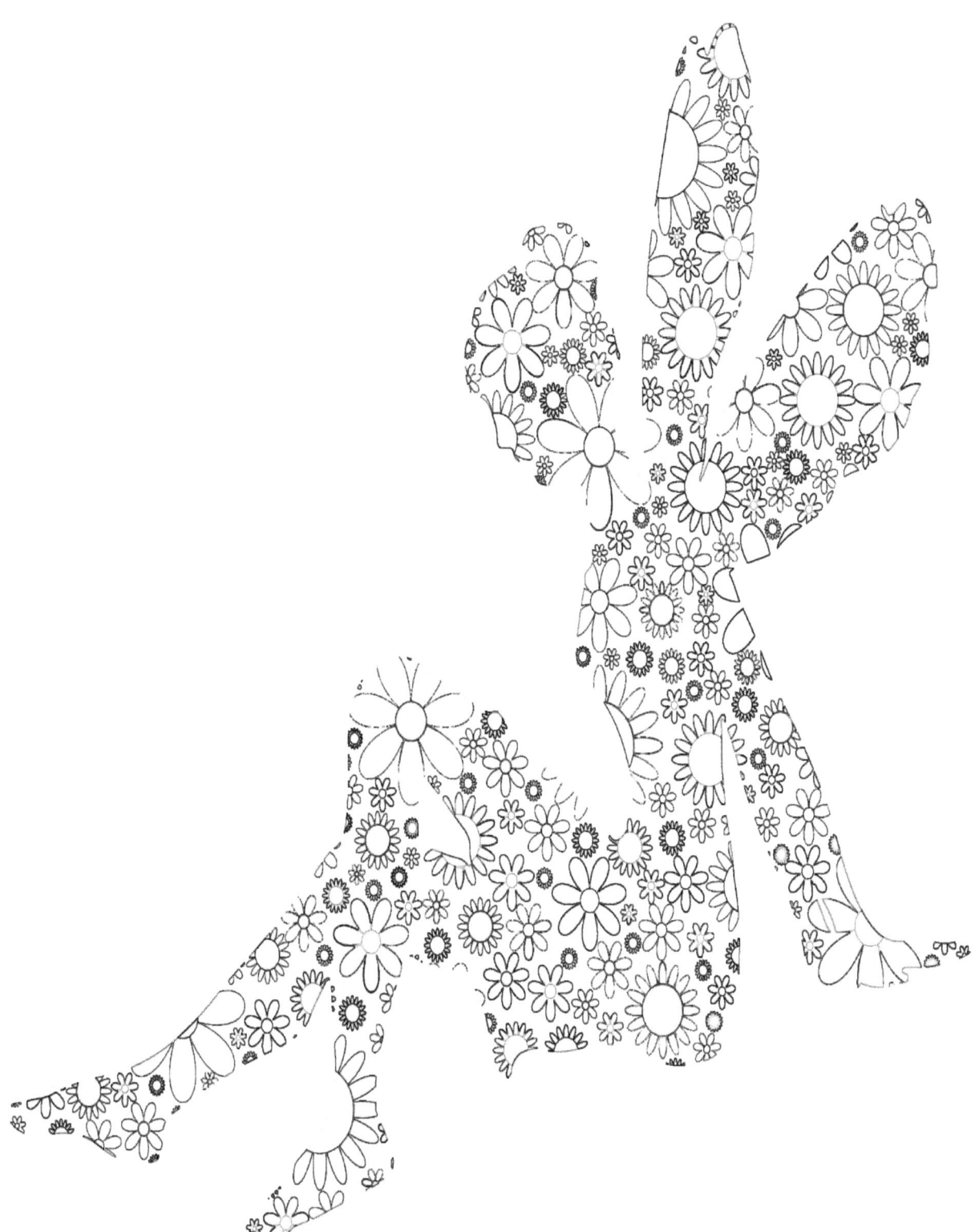

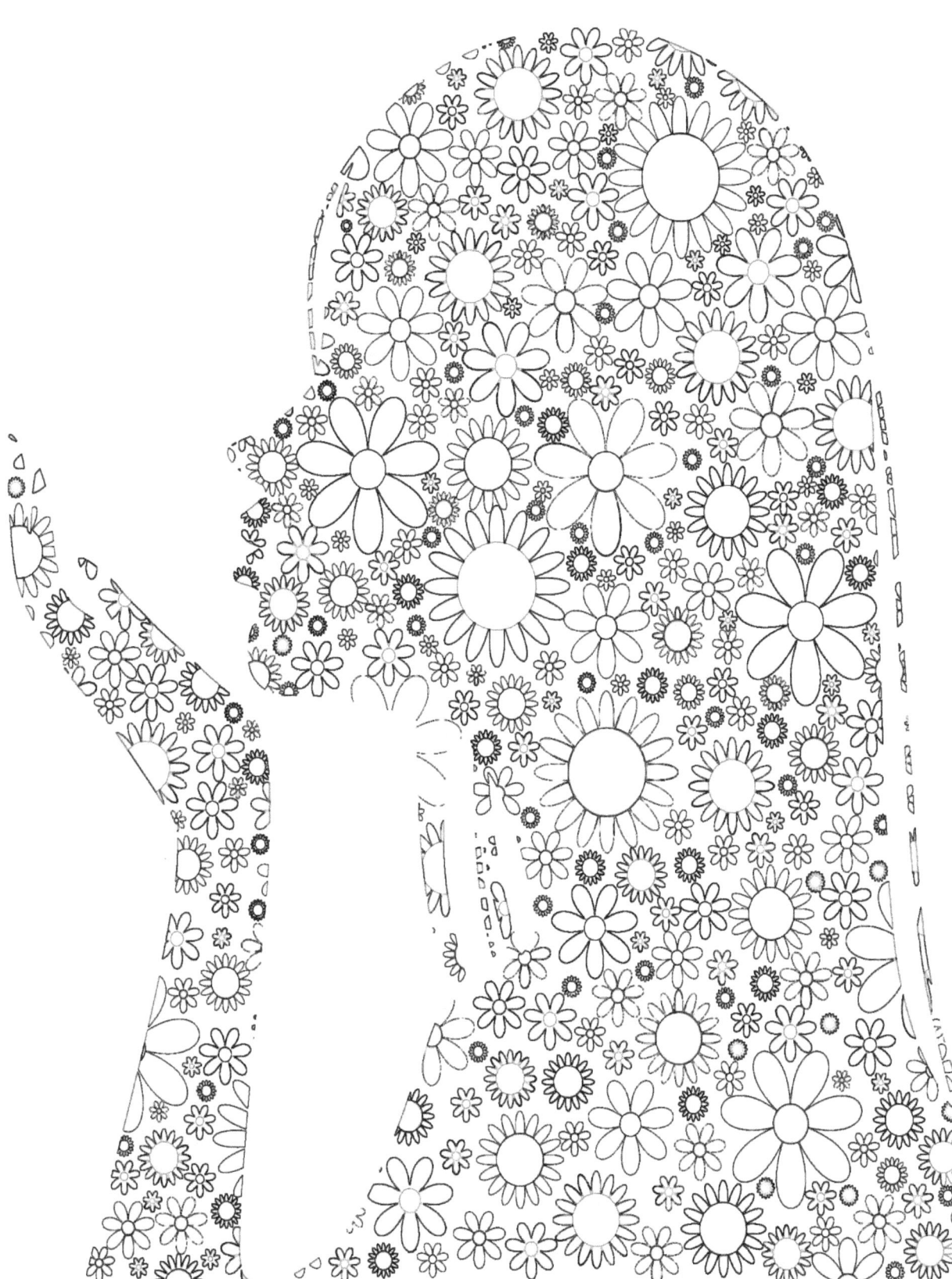

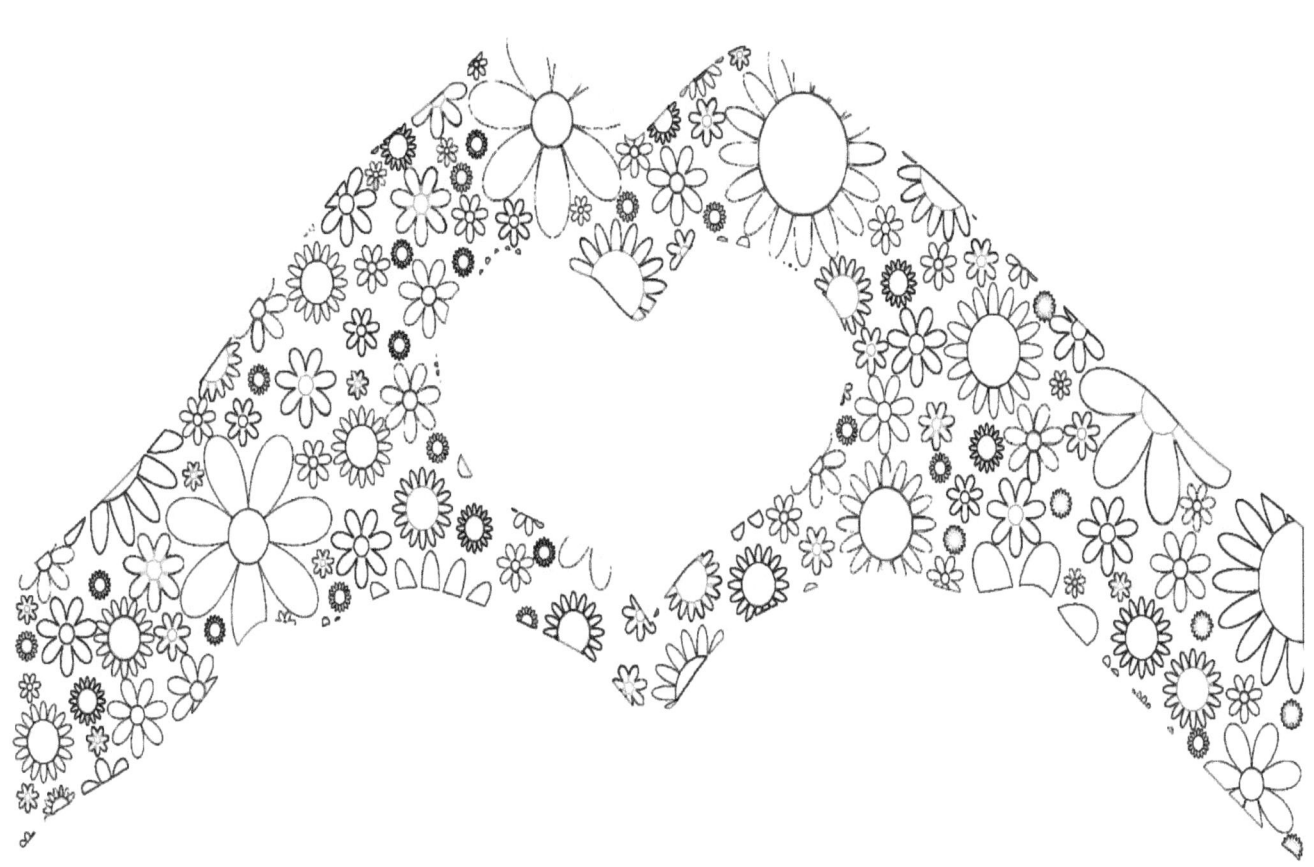

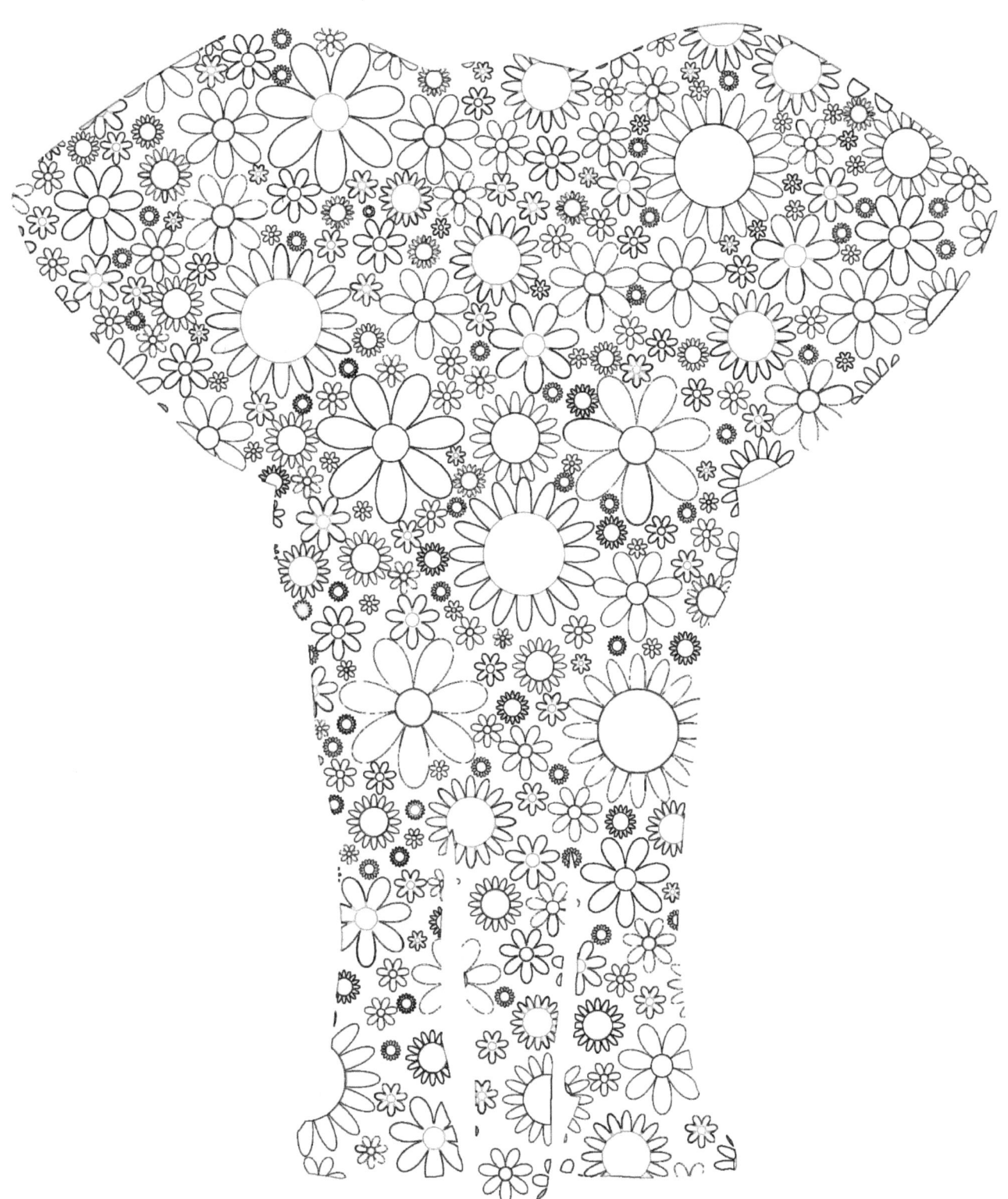

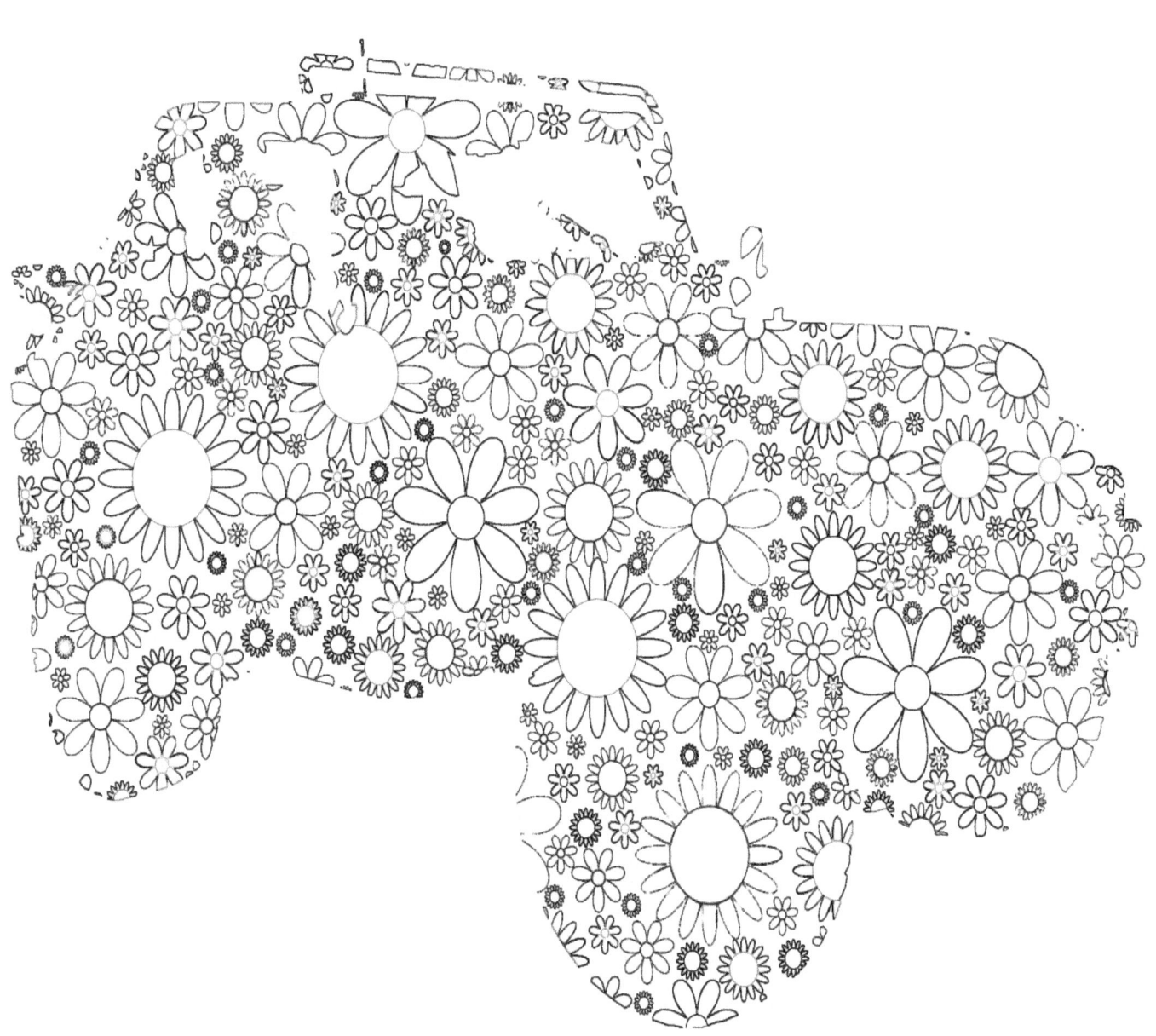

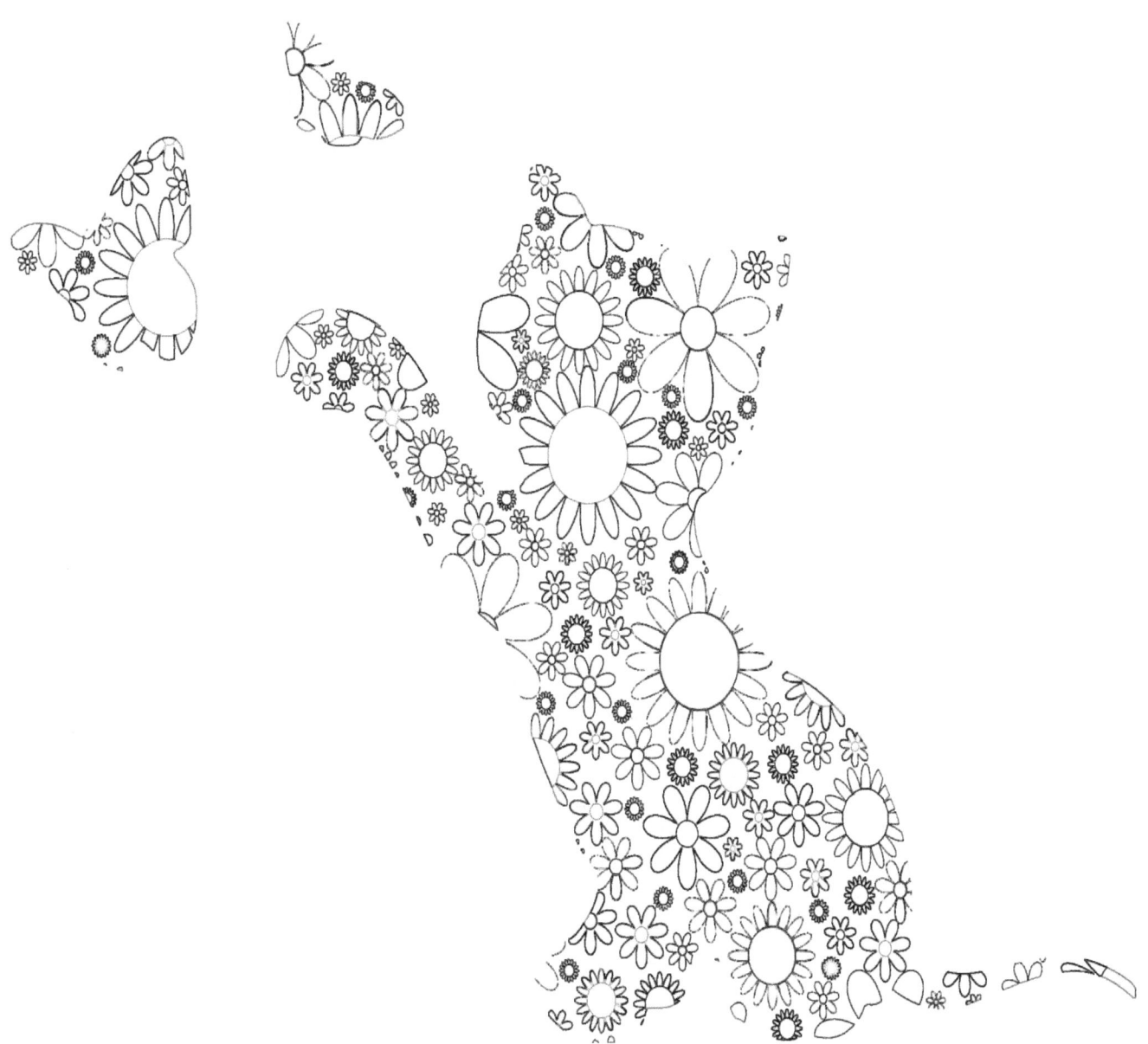

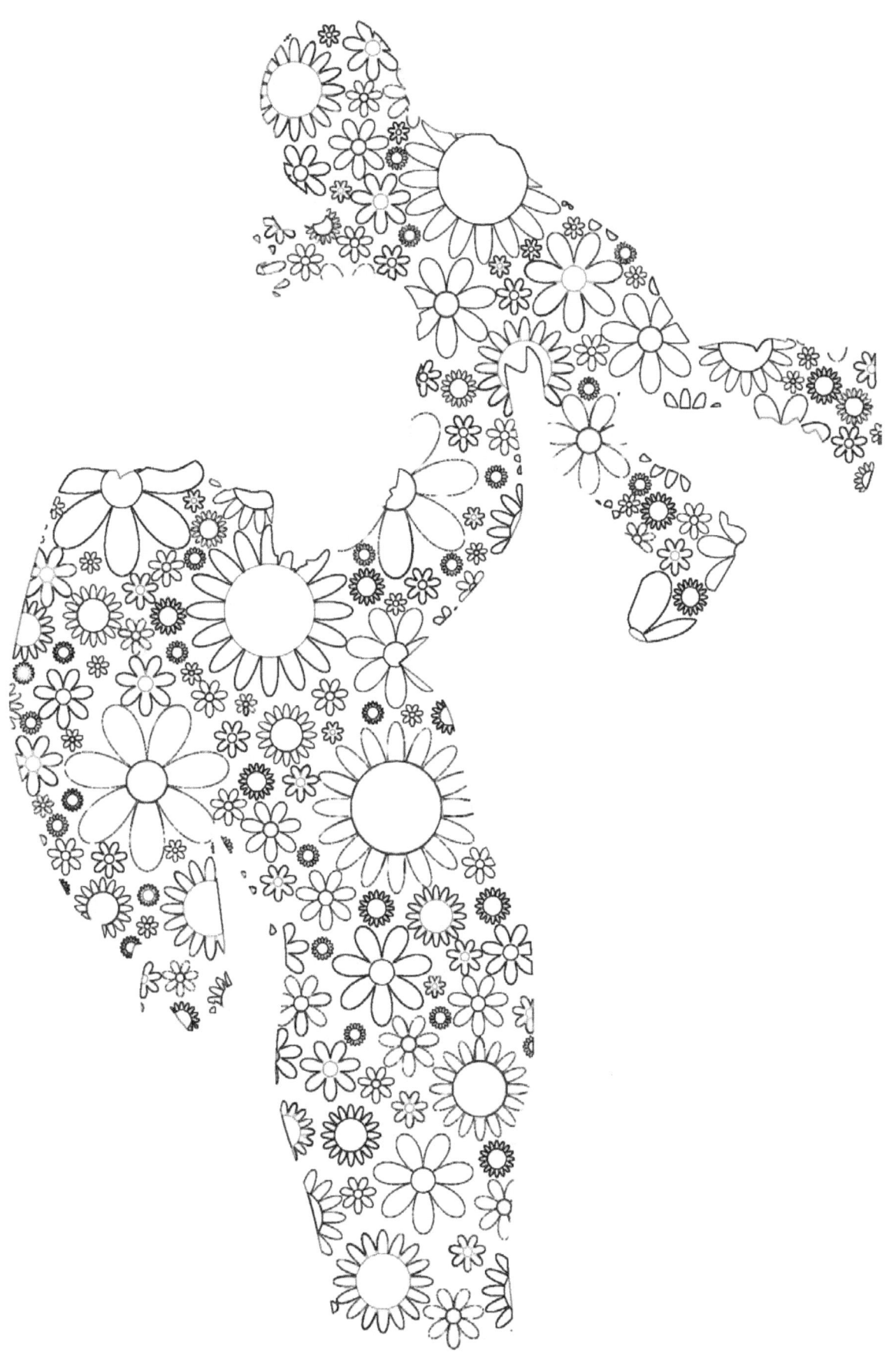

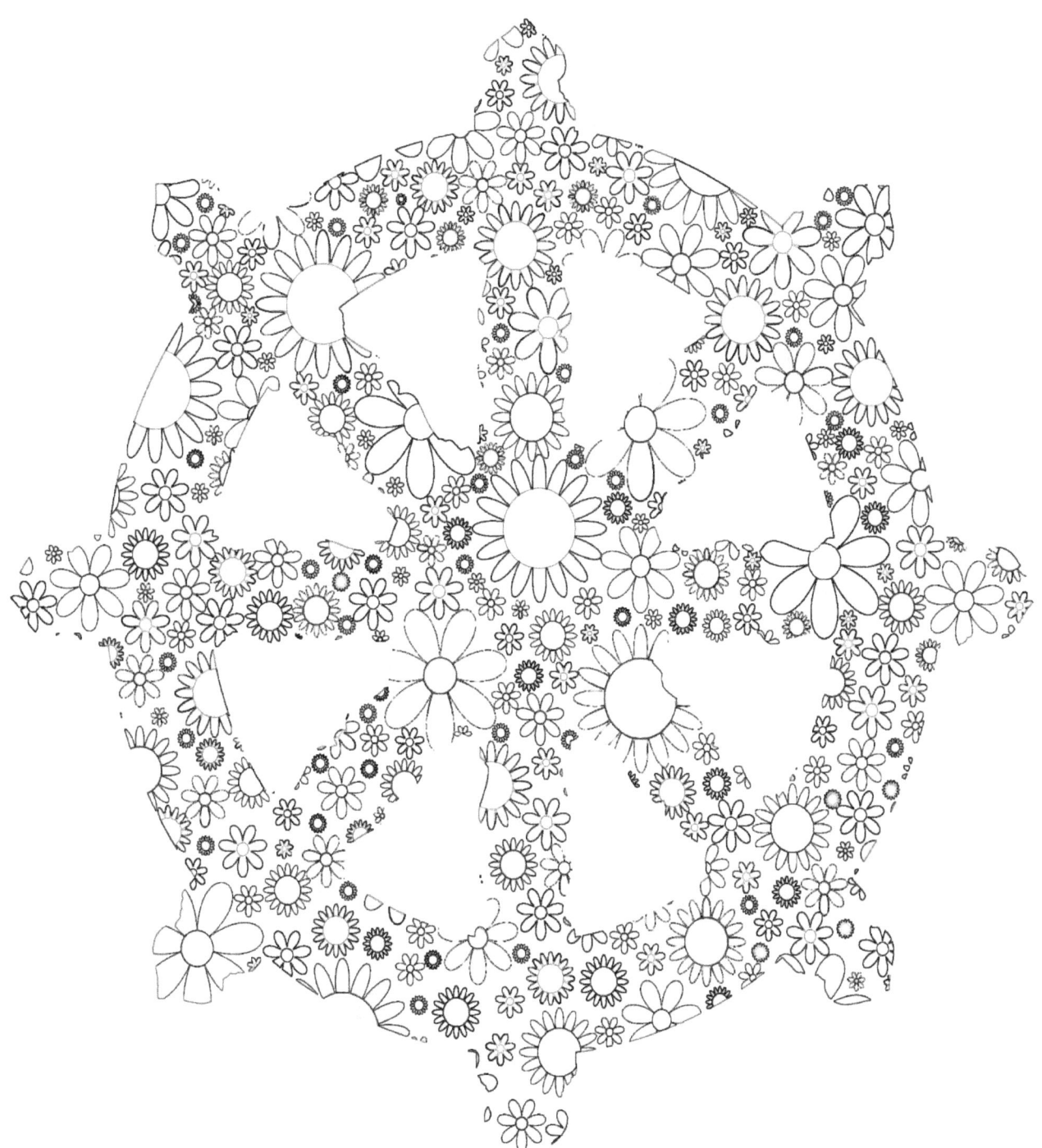

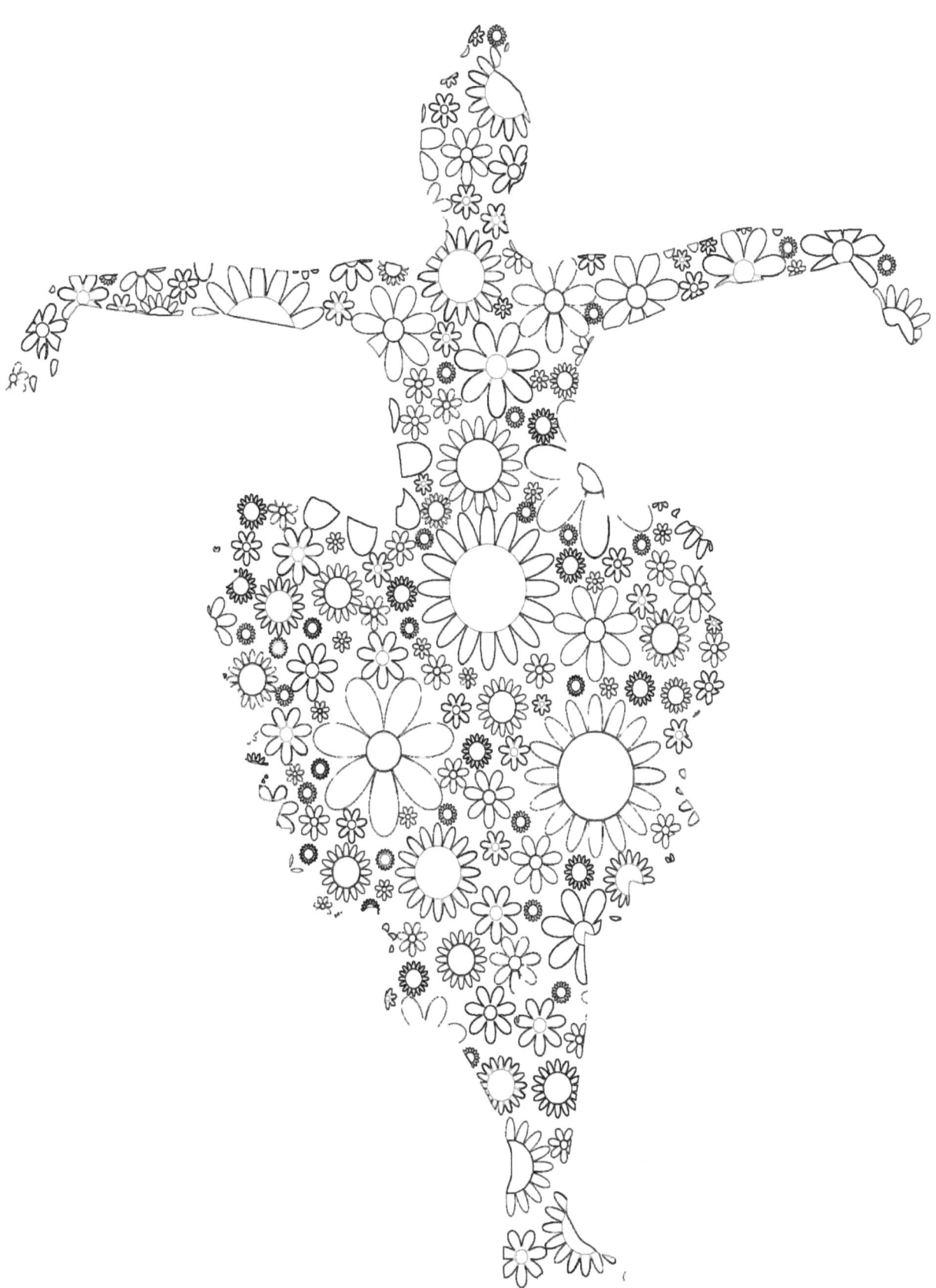

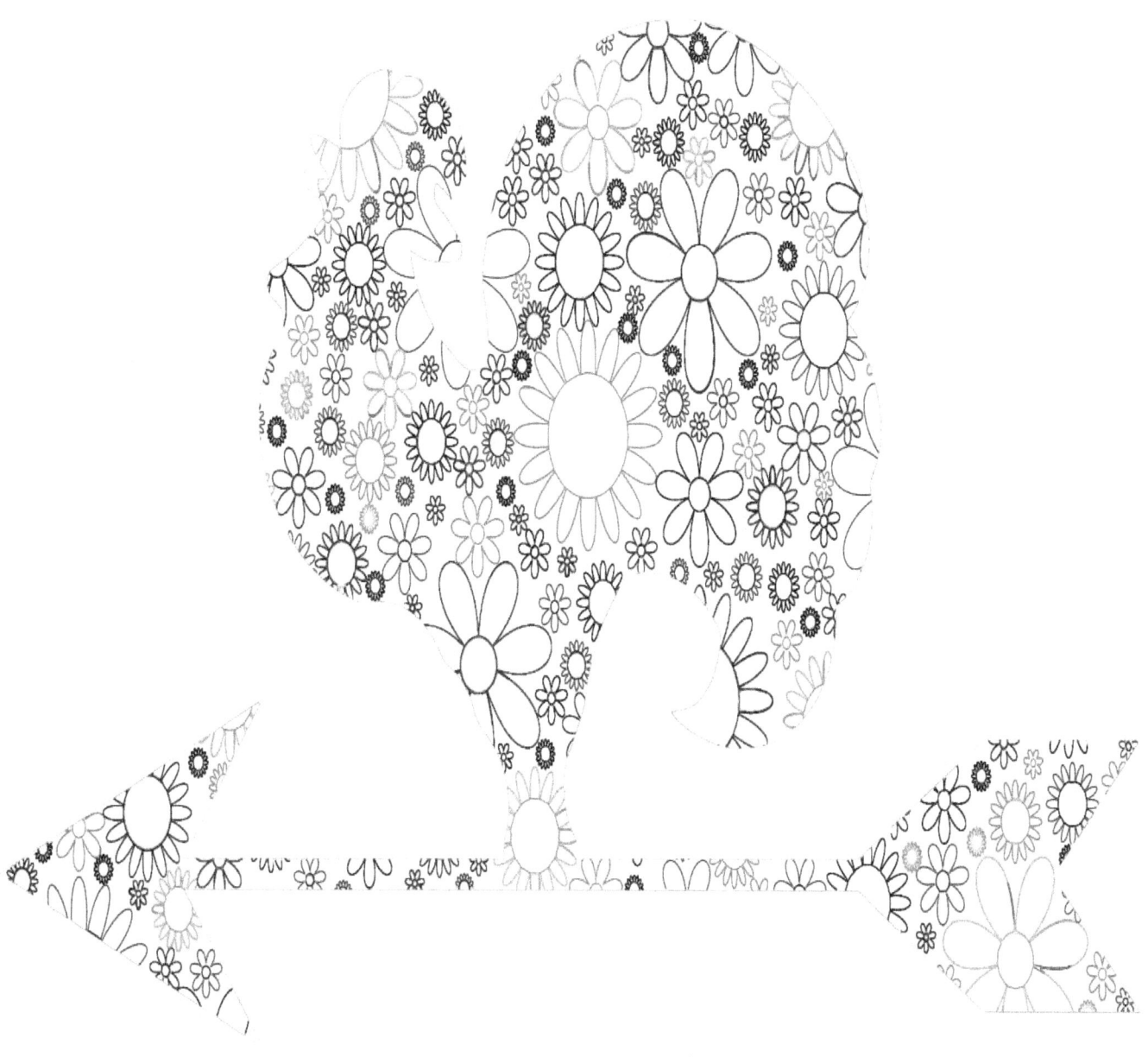

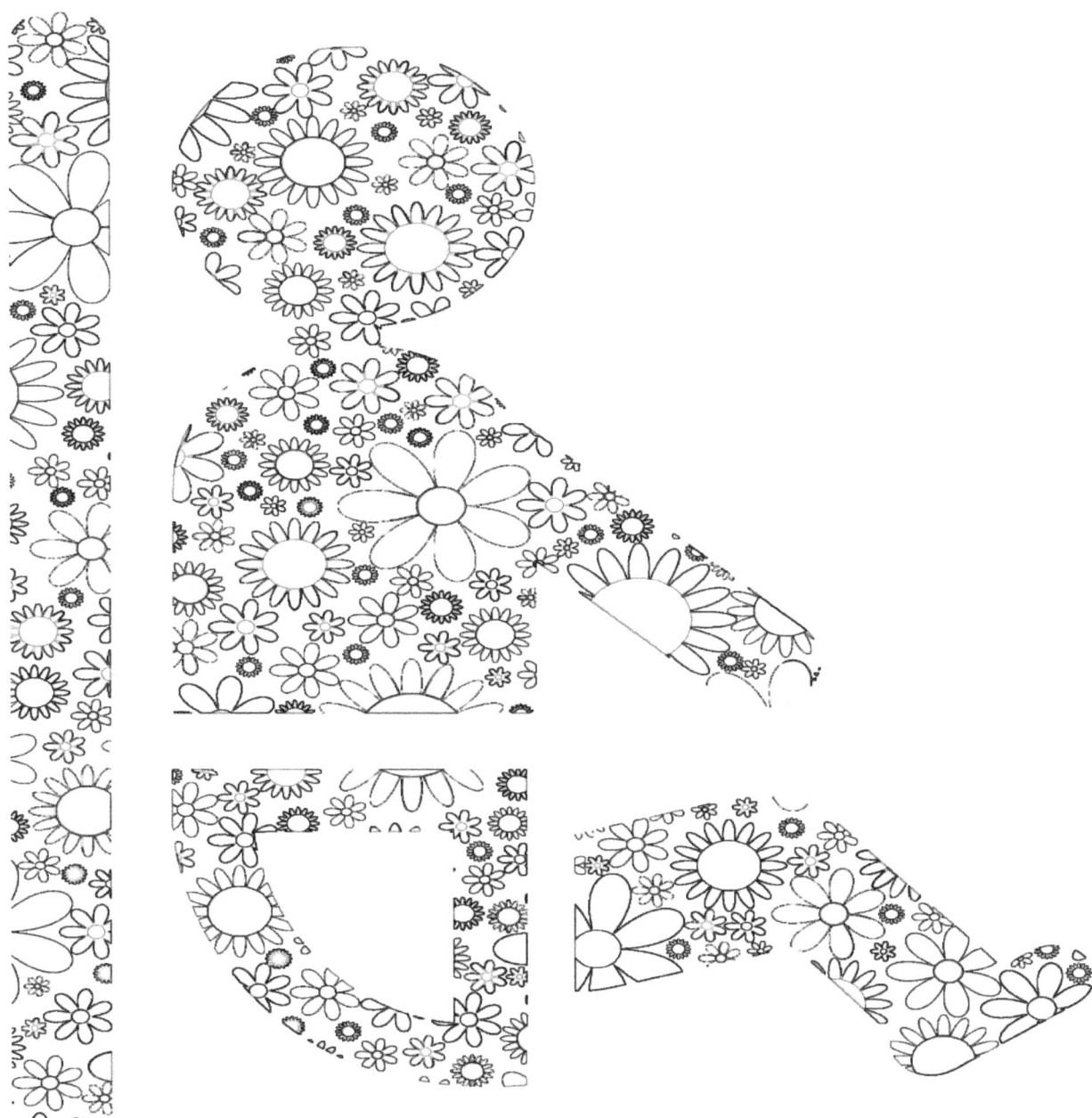

More you may enjoy. Get yours now.

Vase Coloring Book
Dancing Girls Coloring Book
Flowers, Flowers And More Flowers
Adult Coloring Book - Stress Relief
Mandala ~ Stress Relief Adult Coloring Book